UNDERSTANDING DRUGS

Marijuana

TITLES IN THE *UNDERSTANDING DRUGS* SERIES

UNDERSTANDING DRUGS

DRUGS

Marijuana

BRIGID M. KANE

CONSULTING EDITOR
DAVID J. TRIGGLE, PH.D.
University Professor
School of Pharmacy and Pharmaceutical Sciences
State University of New York at Buffalo

CHELSEA HOUSE
An Infobase Learning Company

Chelsea House
An imprint of Infobase Learning
132 West 31st Street
New York NY 10001

Library of Congress Cataloging-in-Publication Data

Kane, Brigid M.
  Marijuana / Brigid M. Kane.
    p. cm — (Understanding drugs)
  Includes bibliographical references and index.
  ISBN-13: 978-1-60413-543-5 (hardcover : alk. paper)
  ISBN-10: 1-60413-543-3 (hardcover : alk. paper)   1. Marijuana.   2. Marijuana
    abuse.   I. Title.
  HV5822.M3M35   2011
  362.29'5—dc22   2011006797

Chelsea House books are available at special discounts when purchased in bulk quantities for businesses, associations, institutions, or sales promotions. Please call our Special Sales Department in New York at (212) 967-8800 or (800) 322-8755.

You can find Chelsea House on the World Wide Web at
http://www.chelseahouse.com

Text design by Kerry Casey
Cover design by Alicia Post
Composition by Newgen
Cover printed by Bang Printing, Brainerd, Minn.
Book printed and bound by Bang Printing, Brainerd, Minn.
Date printed: March 2011
Printed in the United States of America

10 9 8 7 6 5 4 3 2 1

This book is printed on acid-free paper.

All links and Web addresses were checked and verified to be correct at the time of publication. Because of the dynamic nature of the Web, some addresses and links may have changed since publication and may no longer be valid.

Contents

Acknowledgments

The author would like to thank John Zawadzki, Ph.D., for his time, invaluable insights, and critical review of the manuscript. To the high school students who read and commented on the individual chapter manuscripts—thank you, Jonathan Stanyon (Gloversville High School, Gloversville, New York), Carisa Miller (Johnstown High School, Johnstown, New York), and Joseph Kane (Manasquan High School, Manasquan, New Jersey). To Daniel Storto and Desiree Little, Ph.D., thank you for the resources provided and your support. The author is grateful to all her fans (you know who you are) for their encouragement and patience.

foreword

THE USE AND ABUSE OF DRUGS

For thousands of years, humans have used a variety of sources with which to cure their ills, cast out devils, promote their well-being, relieve their misery, and control their fertility. Until the beginning of the twentieth century, the agents used were all of natural origin, including many derived from plants as well as elements such as antimony, sulfur, mercury, and arsenic. The sixteenth-century alchemist and physician Paracelsus used mercury and arsenic in his treatment of syphilis, worms, and other diseases that were common at that time; his cure rates, however, remain unknown. Many drugs used today have their origins in natural products. Antimony derivatives, for example, are used in the treatment of the nasty tropical disease leishmaniasis. These plant-derived products represent molecules that have been "forged in the crucible of evolution" and continue to supply the scientist with molecular scaffolds for new drug development.

Our story of modern drug discovery may be considered to start with the German physician and scientist Paul Ehrlich, often called the father of chemotherapy. Born in 1854, Ehrlich became interested in the ways in which synthetic dyes, then becoming a major product of the German fine chemical industry, could selectively stain certain tissues and components of cells. He reasoned that such dyes might form the basis for drugs that could interact selectively with diseased or foreign cells and organisms. One of Ehrlich's early successes was development of the arsenical "606"—patented under the name *Salvarsan*—as a treatment for syphilis. Ehrlich's goal was to create a "magic bullet," a drug that would target only the diseased cell or the invading disease-causing organism and have no effect on healthy cells and tissues. In this he was not successful, but his great research did lay the groundwork for the successes of the twentieth century, including the discovery of the sulfonamides and the antibiotic penicillin. The latter agent saved countless lives during World War II. Ehrlich, like many scientists, was an optimist. On the eve of World War I, he wrote, "Now that the liability to, and danger of, disease are to a large extent circumscribed—the efforts of chemotherapeutics are directed as far as possible to fill up the gaps left in this ring." As we shall see in the pages of this volume, it is neither the first nor the last time that science has proclaimed its victory over nature, only to have to see this optimism dashed in the light of some freshly emerging infection.

From these advances, however, has come the vast array of drugs that are available to the modern physician. We are increasingly close to Ehrlich's magic bullet: Drugs can now target very specific molecular defects in a number of cancers, and doctors today have the ability to investigate the human genome to more effectively match the drug and the patient. In the next one to two decades, it is almost certain that the cost of "reading" an individual genome will be sufficiently cheap that, at least in the developed world, such personalized medicines will become the norm. The development of such drugs, however, is extremely costly and raises significant social issues, including equity in the delivery of medical treatment.

The twenty-first century will continue to produce major advances in medicines and medicine delivery. Nature is, however, a resilient foe. Diseases and organisms develop resistance to existing drugs, and new drugs must constantly be developed. (This is particularly true for anti-infective and anticancer agents.) Additionally, new and more lethal forms of existing infectious diseases can develop rapidly. With the ease of global travel, these can spread from Timbuktu to Toledo in less than 24 hours and become pandemics. Hence the current concerns with avian flu. Also, diseases that have previously been dormant or geographically circumscribed may suddenly break out worldwide. (Imagine, for example, a worldwide pandemic of Ebola disease, with public health agencies totally overwhelmed.) Finally, there are serious concerns regarding the possibility of man-made epidemics occurring through the deliberate or accidental spread of disease agents—including manufactured agents, such as smallpox with enhanced lethality. It is therefore imperative that the search for new medicines continue.

All of us at some time in our life will take a medicine, even if it is only aspirin for a headache or to reduce cosmetic defects. For some individuals, drug use will be constant throughout life. As we age, we will likely be exposed to a variety of medications—from childhood vaccines to drugs to relieve pain caused by a terminal disease. It is not easy to get accurate and understandable information about the drugs that we consume to treat diseases and disorders. There are, of course, highly specialized volumes aimed at medical or scientific professionals. These, however, demand a sophisticated knowledge base and experience to be comprehended. Advertising on television is widely available but provides only fleeting information, usually about only a single drug and designed to market rather than inform. The intent of this series of books, **Understanding Drugs**, is to provide the lay reader with intelligent, readable, and accurate descriptions of drugs, why and how they are used, their limitations, their side effects, and their future. The series will discuss both *"treatment drugs"*—typically, but not exclusively, prescription drugs, that have well-established criteria of both efficacy and safety—and *"drugs of abuse,"* agents that have pronounced pharmacological and physiological effects but that are, for a variety of reasons, not to be considered for therapeutic purposes. It is our hope that these books will provide readers with sufficient information to satisfy their immediate needs and to serve as an adequate base for further investigation and for asking intelligent questions of health care providers.

—David J. Triggle, Ph.D.
University Professor
School of Pharmacy and Pharmaceutical Sciences
State University of New York at Buffalo

1

Overview of Marijuana

Paul Forge, a research scientist at the Scripps Institute in La Jolla, California, studies the human cardiovascular system in health and disease. He is fascinated by the new developments in the understanding of marijuana's active ingredient, THC, and other cannabinoids, especially the research that shows that these compounds have beneficial as well as harmful effects on the cardiovascular system.

As often happens in academic and clinical research, Paul talked with his colleagues to discuss the numerous seemingly contradictory findings on THC's effects that he's uncovered in his research. He's read that the beneficial effects include prevention of atherosclerosis (the accumulation of fatty deposits in the arteries that lead to high blood pressure) and the prevention of myocardial and cerebral ischemia (impaired blood flow in the heart and brain that can cause heart attack and stroke). He's also read about some serious harmful effects: hypotension (potentially life-threatening drop in blood pressure) due to shock and cardiovascular abnormalities due to cirrhosis (a progressive disease of the liver).

While grabbing lunch with fellow researchers from adjacent laboratories, one colleague handed Paul a paper saying that it might give Paul ideas for his own research projects. Paul smiled later that day when he took out the journal article to read. It was entitled, "Cannabinoids as Therapeutic Agents in Cardiovascular Disease: a Tale of Passions and Illusions."

Neither an herbalist nor a molecular neuroscientist would call marijuana a weed. However, according to the U.S. Department of Agriculture, marijuana,

11

Figure 1.1 Young cannabis plants. *(©Kesu/ shutterstock images)*

or more correctly, the hemp plant, *Cannabis sativa,* is or may become a weedy or invasive plant in all or part of its U.S. range: *Cannabis sativa* tolerates disease, fungus, **mycobacteria**, insects, drought, high and low pH, poor soil, slopes, and weeds.

Marijuana is actually only part of *Cannabis sativa,* the annual plant that contains an enormous number and variety of chemical compounds including 60-plus **cannabinoids**, some of which have **psychoactive**, even hallucinogenic, properties. Marijuana is a green/brown/gray mixture of dried, shredded leaves, mature flowers, buds, stems, and seeds from the *Cannabis sativa* plant, most often the subspecies *Cannabis sativa indica,* which belongs to the Cannabaceae family of flowering herbs originally native to central Asia. The common name for *Cannabis sativa* is the hemp or Indian hemp plant, and very little is wasted with this plant: the stalks and sterilized seeds are widely used as a fiber for cloth and rope, the dried leaves and flowers as an herb (marijuana and hash or hashish), seed oil as vegetable oil (for human

WHAT'S IN A NAME?

marijuana	420	ma
marihuana	skunk	dagga
cannabis	skunkweed	chanvre
hemp	hash	boo
grass	hashish	tea
weed	reefer	mezz
pot	airplane	boom
dope	ganja/ganjah/gunjah	gangster
maryjane	bhang/bhaang	kif
Aunt Mary	charas/churras	rainy day woman

consumption) and for soap, lotion, paints, varnishes, and lamp fuel. Although *Cannabis sativa* has a storied past as one of the oldest cultivated plants, dating back to roughly 4650 B.C., today its cultivation is widespread in temperate regions, nearly worldwide.[1]

The term *marijuana* generally refers to the leaves and other crude plant material of *C. sativa*. Hash or hashish, from unpollinated female plants, is the most potent form of marijuana and is made from the plant resin.

WHY SO POPULAR?

Although the recreational use of marijuana is illegal and carries criminal penalties, marijuana holds a favored status as a popular drug in the United States, Canada, Europe, and most affluent countries. According to the International Narcotics Control Board of the United Nations, marijuana is by far the most commonly used **narcotic** drug: 3% to 4% of the world's population between the ages of 15 and 64 years reported having used marijuana in the past year.[2] Data from the World Health Organization (WHO) reveal the following U.S. incidence rates for lifetime substance use (on at least one occasion): 91.6% for alcohol, 73.6% for tobacco, 42.4% for marijuana, 16.2% for cocaine.[3] The WHO data, collected from a rigorously conducted household survey conducted in 17 countries, support statistics provided by the U.S. Drug Enforcement Agency (part of the U.S. Department of Justice) and the Office of National Drug Control Policy (part of the Office of the President) that report marijuana as the most commonly used illicit drug in the United States. Additionally, marijuana is the largest illicit drug market in terms of global spread of cultivation and volume of production.[4]

Marijuana use appears to be more common among tobacco smokers compared to those who have never used tobacco.[5] Although numerous research studies consistently report this finding of association, other research can be cited to argue the point. Importantly, researchers continue to examine the relationship between the marijuana and tobacco use for a number of reasons, including insights into addictive behaviors and "poly-drug use." Chapter 5 discusses the tracking of marijuana **dependence** rates using detoxification and rehabilitation centers' admission data for persons reporting marijuana use as their sole or primary drug use problem.

Marijuana's popularity is wholly attributable to its narcotic or psychoactive qualities. Marijuana's high is well-known to users and nonusers alike because of the frequency of references to it (e.g., "getting stoned") in popular culture. Marijuana is an intoxicating drug, affecting conscious and unconscious mental processing and all the senses, which are controlled by the **central nervous system** (brain and spinal cord).

Marijuana's appeal is related to one or more of the following feelings experienced by many, but not all, users after smoking marijuana: **euphoria**, reduced anxiety, sense of enhanced well-being, increased sensory perception, increased sociability, heightened sexual experience, and heightened creativity. Other effects, also mediated by the central nervous system, are similar to those associated with alcohol, albeit to varying degrees of drunkenness: unsteady gait, muscle relaxation and/or loss of muscle coordination, weakness, slurred speech, slowed reactions, impaired short-term memory, distortion of time, altered depth perception, fatigue, sedation, **dysphoria**, anxiety, hallucinations, depersonalization (feelings of unreality or strangeness about one's behavior), and disturbed sleep. One unique effect is appetite stimulation, commonly referred to as the "munchies" by marijuana users; this property has actually been exploited to treat **cachexia** (malnutrition or wasting) in HIV/AIDS patients and cancer patients receiving chemotherapy. Other

NARCOTIC DRUGS

The word *narcotic* has a legal meaning as well as a specific scientific meaning; it was originally a medical term restricted to opiates, drugs derived from the sap of the opium poppy plant. *Narcotic* is derived from the Greek word meaning "to numb," as in to deaden or dull the senses. The precise pharmacologic definition of a narcotic is any drug or substance that produces a generalized depression of brain functioning, which manifests as insensibility or stupor. Legally speaking, the term *narcotic* refers to drugs associated with varying degrees of potential for abuse and **addiction**. Note that *narcotic* can be used as an adjective or a noun.

properties of marijuana that have decidedly medical or therapeutic uses are discussed below and in detail in Chapter 7.

Importantly, as with all drugs, dose is key. Low doses of marijuana tend to induce relaxation, disinhibition, and decreased anxiety, whereas high doses typically result in dysphoria, anxiety, and panic attacks, especially in inexperienced users.[6] Low doses tend to increase sensory acuity, usually in a pleasurable way, whereas high doses tend to distort sensory perception and may cause hallucinations and even psychotic episodes. These are typically of short duration, especially if marijuana use is discontinued.

CANNABINOIDS AND MORE

The *Cannabis sativa* plant contains more than 60 chemically related compounds called cannabinoids and more than 400 compounds classified as non-cannabinoids. Non-cannabinoids contained within *Cannibis sativa* plants are chemically diverse, including steroids, vitamins, amino acids, flavonoids, and fatty acids. Scientists are still discovering, isolating, and characterizing some of these compounds (e.g., cannabichromanone derivatives, as described by researchers at the University of Mississippi) and testing them for their individual properties, including potential antimicrobial activity, and possible interactions with one another.[7]

Figure 1.2 Tetrahydrocannibol (THC) crystals visible on marijuana plant. (© Laurin Rinder/ shutterstock images)

Cannabinoids are responsible for the psychoactive properties associated with marijuana (discussed above) as well as the many biological properties that have captured the interest of medical professionals and patients alike—namely, **analgesia** (pain relief), **antiemesis** (for nausea and vomiting), antiproliferative (cancer-fighting), anti-inflammatory (for allergies and infections), and more. However, not all cannabinoids are psychoactive, meaning that some of the cannabinoids do not affect the mind.

The most abundant cannabinoid in the plant is delta-9-tetrahydrocannabinol, more commonly called tetrahydrocannabinol, or **THC**.[8] This is the most active (and most psychoactive) ingredient in the plant and therefore it is the most studied and best characterized cannabinoid compound. It is an interesting historical point that because geographic and climatic conditions, altitude, and latitude affect the content of the pharmacologically active substances in the *C. sativa* plant, in ancient times, not all regions were able to appreciate the plant's drug actions.[9] The THC content of *C. sativa* increases with altitude and is highest in mountainous regions, which explains why the plant's sedative and psychoactive effects were known to people living in the Himalayan mountains of Central Asia and India long before other cultures.

The amount of THC in marijuana has increased significantly since the 1960s. Whereas the typical marijuana cigarette from the 1960s and 1970s contained about 10 mg of THC, marijuana available today (made out of potent *Cannabis sativa* subspecies, e.g., *C. sativa* L. ssp. *indica*) may contain as much as 150 mg of THC.[10] The progressive increase in THC content is thought to be the result of sophisticated genetic breeding and cloning horticulture techniques that can produce high-yield THC plants and improved THC-to-tar ratio in plants, and possibly other advances in cultivation techniques as well.

THC exists in the *C. sativa* plant in the form of tetrahydrocannabinolic acid. It is the heat from the burning of marijuana that converts tetrahydrocannabinolic acid to THC, which is vaporized and then inhaled with the smoke into the lungs.[11] Chapter 3 discusses how THC crosses the cell membranes of the lungs, enters the bloodstream (systemic circulation) through pulmonary capillaries, travels to the heart, and from there to the brain within minutes. The chemistry and biology behind the smoking of marijuana explain the rapid onset of THC's drug action.

In examining trends in marijuana use and abuse, including the frequency of use (e.g., occasional, moderate, regular, or heavy use), social scientists, public health researchers, and others cite the reasons for experimenting with marijuana. There's novelty, risk, peer pressure, social environment factors, and even genetic factors. The controversies and debates about marijuana use are not restricted to social mores, legalities, and policy: Marijuana use represents an emerging public health challenge.

THE DOWNSIDE

Its intoxicating effects are generally what come to mind when discussing marijuana. However, there are adverse effects to smoking marijuana—namely

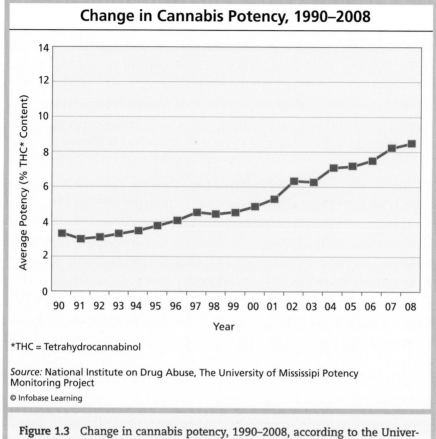

Change in Cannabis Potency, 1990–2008

*THC = Tetrahydrocannabinol

Source: National Institute on Drug Abuse, The University of Mississipi Potency Monitoring Project

© Infobase Learning

Figure 1.3 Change in cannabis potency, 1990–2008, according to the University of Mississippi Potency Monitoring Project sponsored by the National Institute on Drug Abuse.

those that affect the central nervous system, circulatory system, and respiratory system—especially for regular heavy users. THC increases heart rate and modulates blood pressure (lowers blood pressure when standing and increases blood pressure when laying down), and therefore some individuals are at increased risk of a potentially serious cardiovascular event. THC can increase the resistance to blood flow in the cerebral vasculature and therefore there is a risk of stroke. Studies of marijuana-induced adverse effects suggest that chronic stimulation of the receptor molecules that bind to THC (found on the surface of select cells in the body) might influence the production of proteins and other biomolecules involved in maintaining normal physiological processes. For example, higher concentrations of serum apolipoprotein C-III, a known risk factor for cardiovascular disease, were found in heavy marijuana users, compared to control subjects.[12]

The association between marijuana use and seizures, schizophrenia, and psychosis is intriguing and the early observations are now being researched at the structural, molecular, and behavioral levels. New research tools and techniques are able to provide evidence and insights into marijuana's effects on brain structure, memory, and cognitive abilities. Studies have documented that heavy daily marijuana use does damage brain tissue (notably in areas rich in receptors that bind THC) and impair mental health (particularly in individuals with mood disorders, psychosis, or a personal or family history of mental illness).[13] Cognitive deficits include impaired learning, poor retention and retrieval, and perceptual abnormalities. Changes in cognitive abilities may be reversible after discontinuation, except possibly in heavy users (those engaged in heavy daily use spanning long periods). The relationship between marijuana use and schizophrenia is believed to be of a causal nature, one in which marijuana precipitates the onset or relapse of schizophrenia. A scientific basis for the emergence of the myriad central nervous system effects brought on by exposure to THC was summarized in a medical article by an Australian research team: "Exogenous cannabinoids alter the normative functioning of the endogenous cannabinoid system."[14] (The endogenous cannabinoid system refers to those THC-binding receptors found on the surface of different cell types in the body.) Research also shows that there are negative effects of marijuana exposure to fetuses—on brain development, cognitive abilities (e.g., information processing and executive functions), and language development.[15]

Drug dependence and addiction can develop depending on frequency and duration of marijuana use and genetics and personality of the user. Physical dependence refers to the emergence of discernable and measurable **withdrawal** symptoms upon abrupt cessation of a drug (e.g., flulike symptoms, restlessness, fever, and chills). Marijuana dependence occurs in about 7% to 10% of regular users, with early age of onset of use and heavy frequency of use (weekly or daily) as strong predictors of future dependence.[16] Table 1.1 catalogs the negative health consequences associated with chronic heavy marijuana use and/or those seen in individuals with predisposing risk factors or conditions.

Table 1.1. Adverse effects induced or exacerbated by marijuana	
• Chronic inflammation (different organs and tissues)	• Human papilloma virus (HPV) infection
• Lung cancer	• Psychosis
• Pulmonary airway obstructive disease	• Schizophrenia
• Oral cancer	• Depression
• Mood disorders	• Memory impairment
• Stroke	• Seizures
• Transient ischemia	• Cardiovascular disease
• Dependence and addiction	• Myocardial infarction

In addition to the concern that marijuana use can lead to addiction, social scientists also debate whether marijuana use leads to the use, misuse, and abuse of other drugs. The idea that the use of an addictive substance leads to the use of other more addictive and more harmful drugs is not new. However, the growing advocacy for legalizing or decriminalizing marijuana has put this hypothesis in the spotlight again.

Some studies have shown that the gateway progression of drug use is a common pattern in drug-using teens. That is, there is a progression from legal substance use, such as tobacco and/or alcohol, to illegal marijuana use, to so-called harder drugs. These studies have shaped prevention efforts and government policy for decades. However, other equally valid studies provide evidence that this is not the only pattern, and that marijuana use is not a requirement for progression to hard drugs. In fact, the reverse pattern (illicit to licit drug use) has been found, and individuals exhibiting this pattern were no more likely to abuse drugs than those who follow the gateway pattern.[17]

Addiction experts agree that marijuana use is not as serious a public health problem as other drugs of abuse such as cocaine, heroin, and methamphetamine. Nevertheless, there is concern that the availability of more potent marijuana (marijuana with higher THC content) has increased addiction

Figure 1.4   Marijuana leaf, paper joint, and hashish, or the concentrated resin from female marijuana plants.   *(© Kandelaki/ shutterstock)*

rates and is potentially more dangerous to teenagers, whose brains are still developing.

IS MARIJUANA MEDICINE?

THC and other cannabinoids in marijuana have beneficial effects in certain disease states, including acute and chronic pain, malnutrition and wasting, **glaucoma**, **autoimmunity**, and neurodegenerative diseases like **multiple sclerosis** and **Alzheimer's disease**. Researchers have long recognized that cannabinoids possess anti-inflammatory and anticancer activities. The precise mechanism of action in specific pathological conditions is known for some but not all cannabinoids. Chapter 3 discusses how THC produces such therapeutic benefits as pain relief, and Chapter 7 provides information on the use of plant-derived and chemically synthesized THC as medical treatments for specific pain conditions, such as persistent and unrelenting pain that is unresponsive to morphine and other strong analgesics, as well as other

MEDICAL MARIJUANA: FOLK MEDICINE?

Herbs, balms, aromatherapy, witches' brews, snake oil, marijuana. To some people, all of these fall into one category—sham. Is the use of marijuana as medicine a sham? Not at all. With the discovery of the cannabinoid system, which consists of naturally occurring cannabinoids in the body and complementary THC-binding receptors on the surface of select cells, scientists have demonstrated specific physiologic effects as a direct consequence of binding between cannabinoids and cannabinoid receptors. But smoking as a method of ingesting marijuana is where scientists draw the line: Inhaling tar and other carcinogenic materials into the lungs is something that those devoted to healing cannot advocate. However, the American Medical Association, the American College of Physicians, and numerous other professional heath care organizations allow that, until a smokeless rapid-onset inhalation delivery system or another safe and reliable delivery system is developed, smoked marijuana does hold modest clinical benefit for a small patient population for whom conventional medications are ineffective.

Amid the controversy over medical marijuana, medicinal chemists, pharmacologists, and molecular biologists are continuing to investigate alternative routes of administration for plant-derived and synthetic cannabinoids, and right now, the search is on find *the* cannabinoid—*the* molecule—with potent and selective affinity for one or more cannabinoid receptors and all the right pharmacologic properties. But that just scratches the surface. The quest continues for an as yet unidentified substance that controls the synthesis and release of cannabinoids in the body.

conditions and diseases. Health care professionals, researchers, patients, policy makers, and laypeople have all pointed out that marijuana—and therefore cannabinoids—may have not have any real therapeutic benefit, but that patients report improvement because of the induced euphoria and their feeling-no-pain state of mind. Perhaps. The Institute of Medicine, a public health and policy think tank chartered by the National Academy of Sciences, acknowledged such opinion and recommends that the issue merits scientific evaluation:[18]

> Psychological effects of cannabinoids such as anxiety reduction and sedation, which can influence medical benefits, should be evaluated in clinical trials. The psychological effects of cannabinoids are probably important determinants of their potential therapeutic value. They can influence symptoms indirectly which could create false impressions of the drug effect or be beneficial as a form of adjunctive therapy.

2
History of Marijuana

Juan was used to farm work, from sunup to sundown in the hot dusty dry fields of California's Ojai Valley. He had been working steadily alongside family and extended family, rather contentedly, for 15 years. Juan and his family had emigrated from Mexico in 1920, fleeing the revolution there, looking to start a new life where there was plenty of work. Like other Mexicans, Juan's family brought little with them to the United States: a limited food supply for their journey, the clothes they wore, and whatever else they could carry. Juan's family lived and worked with other Mexican immigrant families in California and they frequently ate together. After the supper meal, at dusk or after dark, Juan would relax before going to sleep with other tired field workers by smoking leaves from the Cannnibus sativa plant. It was a ritual that was typically low-key. Not so at the feasts.

Once a month, for special feasts, the community came together and enjoyed traditional Mexican foods, songs, and dance. The all-day and all-night celebrations included alcohol and marijuana and tobacco cigarettes. Marijuana smoking did different things to each smoker. A couple of Juan's cousins would get loud and rowdy, and all too often pick fights and get into trouble. Like clockwork, the sheriff and his men would come around when they were notified that someone was seriously hurt. The local law enforcement became familiar with Mexican feast days and traditions, and they would be prepared to step in when things got out of control. Tensions were building, and rumors were circulating about possible laws that would prohibit marijuana smoking *because of the escalating violence. There was also talk of a marijuana tax, which would have the same effect (making it prohibitive to afford marijuana). Sure enough, two years later, Juan learned of the Marihuana Tax Act of 1937.*

Attempting to pinpoint the origin of man's discovery or use of marijuana is akin to trying to identify the beginning of time. Scientists are still on the trail of both endeavors, and most likely will be for a long time. It is known that the ancient Egyptians, Assyrians, Chinese, Indians, Greeks, Persians (including Sythians and Iranians), and Moroccans have used marijuana in numerous ways for thousands of years.

Botanists have identified *Cannabis sativa* plant parts found in a grave dating back to around 4000 B.C. in the Turfan Depression in the Xinjiang Uyghur Autonomous Region of China, near the Gobi desert. Inhabitants of this region in central Asia have been described in Chinese records as nomadic peoples with light hair and blue eyes (Caucasians) speaking an Indo-European language possibly related to Celtic, Italic, and Anatolic languages. The Chinese writings about these people—the Gūshī culture (later the Jūshi, or Cheshi)—dates to 3950 B.C. Genetic and chemical experiments on the well-preserved plant parts from the excavated tombs, completed in 2007, provide conclusive evidence that *C. sativa* existed in 4650 B.C. in this region. Botanic evidence of the sizable quantity of plant material found in the tomb (789 grams of pounded female-only plant parts, without any stalks or branches) suggests that *C. sativa* was cultivated and not merely gathered from wild plants by this nomadic people. Because the female plant parts contain more THC and other psychoactive cannabinoids, the botanical experts involved in the study of this plant sample suggest that the *C. sativa* plant was cultivated in 4650 B.C. for its psychoactive properties and for medicinal and possibly divinatory purposes. These researchers support their hypothesis by pointing out the lack of stalks and branches, which strongly suggests that the 789 gram sample represents not one plant but the collection of plant parts from a field of plants.[1]

The consensus is that marijuana originated in central Asia, but from there, the trail is not so clear. Indirect evidence of the use of woven hemp in the Neolithic Yangshao culture (4200 to 3200 B.C.), along the Yellow River, in the Honan province of China, comes from cord impressions on pottery from that era. Direct evidence from the Bronze Age oasis civilization of central

MARIJUANA'S ORIGIN IN CENTRAL ASIA

"Central Asia, a vast land of deserts, steppes and oases is, despite its name, usually seen as of marginal historical influence, a kind of cultural vacuum between the great civilizations of China to the east, India to the south and the Middle East to its west. Yet, very early on, thriving trade routes passed through the region and these became known as the Silk Roads, on account of the importance of Chinese silk for both Muslim and Western merchants . . . Central Asia was an important centre for the transmission of new discoveries and religious ideas from prehistoric times onwards. The hemp plant, being of major technological importance as a fibre and being one of the most influential psychoactive plants in human culture, was most likely a key trade item from a very early date."
—Richard Rudgley, "Cannabis," *The Encyclopedia of Psychoactive Substances*. New York: Thomas Dunne Books, 1998.

Asia (ancient Margiana or current-day Turkmenistan), dating back to 2200 to 1700 B.C., comes from preserved marijuana flowers and seeds that have been excavated from sites in this area. Archeological evidence shows that hemp was used in ancient China for its strength as a fiber to make rope, bowstrings (for agricultural and military purposes), thread, textiles, fishnets, sailcloth, and paper. Pieces of hemp cloth have been traced to the Western Zhou era of ancient China (approximately 1050–700 B.C.), which is about the same time that Indo-Europeans were settling in India. In addition to cordage and cloth, the *C. sativa* plant was also likely used in ancient China for its psychoactive and medicinal properties, and in the ancients' spiritual life as well. Historians, archeologists, linguists, and cultural anthropologists have evidence and artifacts from numerous Chinese cultures indicating the use of hemp—and to a much lesser extent the use of marijuana vapors, which may have been reserved for shamanic purposes. Smoked marijuana appears to have been much more prominent in societies of the Middle East and India.[2]

Hindi and Sanskrit literature of India from approximately 1500 B.C. contains references to the use of marijuana possibly as a ritualistic offering and a way of communing with the gods. Medicinal use of marijuana by the Indian

Figure 2.1   Mural of an Indian holy man with pipe for smoking hash (Rajasthan, North India, undated).   (© *imagebroker/ Alamy*)

Buddhists goes as far back as 250 B.C., although no written record exists. An ancient Persian religious text of Zoroastrianism dating to about 600 B.C. mentions what some scholars believe is a reference to the medical use of marijuana. (Zoroastrianism is an ancient pre-Islamic religion that survives in isolated areas of Iran and India.) The Assyrians in Mesopotamia and Assyria (modern Iraq) used marijuana to relieve sorrow and grief.[3]

    C. sativa has been used in many places worldwide throughout history—from central Asia to China and southern Siberia, to India and Southeast Asia, to western Asia and the Middle East, to sub-Saharan Africa, Europe, and eventually the Americas. Its economic, medicinal, religious, ritualistic, and recreational value and uses appear to have been appreciated by practically all civilizations in all eras beginning around 4500 B.C.[4]

MARIJUANA AND THE WEST

C. sativa was known for its use as a fiber in Greece as early as 270 B.C., and its use traveled to France and Europe, but few historical records note marijuana's use as a psychoactive drug in Europe.[5] Hemp seeds are thought to have reached the Americas from Europe in the 1500s.[6] Native Americans such as the Iroquois appeared to have used *C. sativa* as a stimulant and medically to convince patients that they had recovered.[7] *C. sativa* seeds reached South America around the same time with African slaves, with evidence pointing to Angolan slaves in particular because of the adoption of marijuana's use in religious rituals to gods including Angolan deities; also, the origin of words for marijuana in Brazil (*maconha, diamba, liamba*) derives from the Angolan language.[8]

    Hemp was a highly valued cash crop in the American colonies where it was used for agriculture, textile, maritime, and military purposes. Connecticut, Massachusetts, and Virginia enacted laws in the early 1600s requiring colonists to grow hemp.[9] Marijuana's use as a recreational drug in the Americas is not recorded until the mid-1800s, coinciding with the discovery of marijuana's intoxicating effects in European society and its therapeutic benefits heralded by English, Irish, and French physicians. American doctors joined their European colleagues in studying and adopting the use of powders, poultices, balms, tinctures, and other extracts of *C. sativa* for numerous ailments. The use of marijuana as a medicine began declining as early as the late 1800s in Europe and the United States for two main reasons: (1) because of

Figure 2.2 Spreading harvested hemp in nineteenth-century Kentucky.
(© The Filson History Society/ Library of Congress)

the inconsistent and unreliable dosages and hence the problems encountered with prescribing specific products and doses for individual patient's needs, and (2) because other, more effective and reliable medicines became available, including aspirin and opiates.[10] The last entry for marijuana tinctures and extracts in medicinal pharmaceutical manuals of Europe and the United States was in the 1930s and 1940s.

MARIJUANA IN THE UNITED STATES: FROM PROHIBITION TO THE PRESENT

Students of American history hear "prohibition" and thoughts of bootleg alcohol, underground distilleries, and speakeasy clubs come to mind. The Prohibition era in the United States (1920–1932) restricted the popular use of alcohol: the manufacture, import, export, transportation, and sale of alcoholic beverages were illegal. However, at the same time, marijuana was being introduced into American popular culture. Marijuana use in social settings as an intoxicant appears to have originated in Texas, Southern California, and the Southwest in the early 1900s, probably around 1910, as Mexican immigrants

Figure 2.3 French lithograph depicting two men smoking hashish, 1845. (© akg-images / Maurice Babey/ Newscom)

drifted north due to the Mexican Revolution. The temperance movement in the United States, which actually took hold before the Civil War, was originally a crusade against alcohol consumption, promulgating abstinence. By the mid-1930s, this movement opposed the use of marijuana as well.[11]

Criminalization of marijuana in the United States dates back to 1930, with the creation of the U.S. Federal Bureau of Narcotics (predecessor of the

REEFER MADNESS: A CULT CLASSIC

Just before the Marijuana Tax Act of 1937, the original film *Reefer Madness* was released as a propaganda piece sponsored by the U.S. government, portraying the evils of marijuana (reefer) and discouraging

(continues)

Figure 2.4.   Still from *Reefer Madness.*   (National Library of Medicine)

(continued)

its use. The timing of the black-and-white film's release in 1936 says it all.

The plot of the film tells the story of a fictional young couple who entice the local high school teens to smoke marijuana at their wild parties. They become addicted and the lives of all involved with marijuana are inevitably shattered; one teen is the driver of a hit-and-run, another is killed in a fight over a gun, and others slowly go insane.

The movie was released as a colorized version in 2004 with new added special effects. The colorized version intentionally features unrealistic color schemes such as the appearance of smoke from marijuana as green, blue, orange, and purple, reflecting each smoker's mood and their different level of intoxication or addiction. This film version played with the coded language of pot users, including "420": during the film, the number "2," followed by the number "40," was flashed across the screen very briefly and very quickly. This sequence of numbers was a joke on subliminal messages, referring to 420, which is slang for marijuana. Some sources indicate that the release date of the film (April 20) was also a play on the drug culture slang.

current U.S. Drug Enforcement Agency). Individual state laws were on the books by 1931 and the federal Marijuana Tax Act of 1937 required all persons using marijuana or possessing *C. sativa* to register and pay a tax (a lower tax rate was applied for medical use versus all other uses).[12]

World War II created a need for hemp when international trade from Asia was severely curtailed or cut off completely by the Japanese. Thus *C. sativa* cultivation was legalized and domestic hemp production was used for twine, rope, canvas, soldiers' boots, and myriad other military and industrial purposes. In 1942, the U.S. Department of Agriculture issued *Hemp for Victory,* a film promoted to farmers to cultivate hemp to support the war effort. By 1945, *C. sativa* cultivation by U.S. farmers was back to pre-wartime levels.

The taxing and eventual banning of marijuana in the United States narrowed the recreational use of the drug in open society, and by so doing perhaps elevated its appeal to intellectuals and artists in various circles, including

Hollywood. Some social historians note that marijuana's use in the period up to the 1950s was highest in black and Hispanic immigrant neighborhoods.[13] It could be argued that the temperance movement, the laws, and policies might be responsible for driving marijuana to an underground status and creating the black market that still exists today. Harry J. Anslinger, the first commissioner of the Federal Bureau of Narcotics from 1930 to 1962, did not succeed in squelching marijuana's popular recreational use. Marijuana held a central position in national discussions and debates (alongside such topics as communism and morality) in the second half of the twentieth century. Marijuana's consumption was highest during this period due largely to the noise made by the antiestablishment generation of the 1950s and 1960s as they fought government and authority figures for their right to smoke pot for its euphoric and calming properties.[14] The 1960s represent the height of marijuana's popularity in the United States (in conjunction with hippies, rock-and-roll, free love, Woodstock, flower power, and flower children). However, marijuana's use and abuse since the 1960s was not limited to the United States, and indeed marijuana's popularity soared in developed countries in North America, Western Europe, and Australia throughout the 1970s.

3
Cannabinoid Chemistry and Pharmacology

Tim started smoking pot while he was in eighth grade. Through high school and in college, getting high became part of his everyday lifestyle. At the age of 20, Tim began to experience symptoms of fever, fatigue, rash, as well as headaches. Not long after that flulike period, Tim noticed sores in his mouth and bleeding, bad enough or strange enough to make him see a doctor. After a thorough exam and medical history, the doctor diagnosed Tim with a fungal infection of the mouth (candidiasis), which is a known opportunistic infection in persons with a compromised immune system, like cancer patients, transplant recipients, and those with HIV infection. Tim was tested and learned that he was HIV positive.

After his diagnosis and after learning more about HIV infection and AIDS, Tim became depressed and smoked pot more frequently. His doctor's office gave him a lot of information about HIV/AIDS drugs, and he started a drug regimen—a cocktail of three drugs that cripple HIV and prevent the virus from multiplying. Shortly after beginning the regimen, Tim began to experience hallucinations and he became paranoid. Tim was scared enough to reach out to his doctor and tell him what was happening and he decided that he should probably let the doctor know about his pot smoking. Tim was candid with his doctor, revealing his daily habit and long pot-smoking history. Blood tests were ordered to measure the level of the HIV/AIDS drugs because the THC in pot can affect the metabolism of other drugs in the body and possibly exacerbate their side effects. The doctor put Tim in touch with a counseling service and referred him to a drug treatment facility for his marijuana use. The doctor also switched one of the drugs in Tim's HIV/AIDS cocktail treatment with a different drug that does not inter- act with THC.

Like all drugs, the effects of marijuana can be traced to the chemical com- position and molecular structure of the active ingredients. Tetrahydrocan- nabinol, or THC, one of the 60-plus cannabinoid compounds found in the *Cannabis sativa* plant, is marijuana's main active ingredient. Scientists predict and test the effects of THC's on the body by studying the chemical nature and reactivity of all of the atoms positioned as they are in the THC molecule and the potential chemical interactions between the atoms in the THC molecule and the atoms of select biomolecules in the blood and other tissues in the body. The chemical and physical properties of THC (e.g., **solubility**, stability, reactivity) as well as the compound's pharmacologic properties (e.g., absorp- tion, metabolism, elimination, dose-response effect), are also critical pieces of information. Scientists harness all available **pharmacodynamic** and **phar- macokinetic** tools to analyze marijuana's "high" in terms of the drug's effects on a biological system, which include increased pulse rate, decreased blood pressure, muscle weakness, increased appetite, change in perception, and euphoria.[1] Numerous factors determine how a drug acts in the body, includ- ing its route of administration. For example, marijuana's effects can be dimin- ished or heightened depending on whether THC is inhaled, ingested as a pill, or administered as a mouth spray, **transdermal** patch, or rectal enema. Other factors include **dosage** and interaction with foods or other drugs ingested or administered within the same time frame.

As discussed below, the chemical structure or spatial arrangement of atoms in the THC molecule can explain the different properties of THC in the laboratory and in the body. Once THC was isolated in the laboratory and its structure revealed in 1964,[2] the field of cannabinoid research went into high gear. Chemists, biochemists, and pharmacologists could finally inves- tigate the properties of the primary active ingredient of marijuana and other cannabinoids based on chemistry (atoms, electrical charges, affinities, radi- cals, bonds, and reactions).

PHARMACODYNAMICS AND PHARMACOKINETICS: THE TWO BRANCHES OF PHARMACOLOGY

Pharmacodynamics: How a drug acts on the body. Pharmacodynamics describes drug action as a quantitative relationship: dose-effect response (how much drug produces how much effect). For many drugs, as the dose of a drug is increased the response to the drug increases, a phenomenon represented graphically as a dose-response curve.

Pharmacokinetics: How a drug moves through the body. Following administration of a drug, the body immediately begins to work on the drug. Pharmacokinetics describes how the body works on a drug from the time it is administered: the processes of absorption, distribution to various tissues (e.g., bone, brain), metabolism, and elimination.

THC CHEMICAL COMPOSITION AND STRUCTURE

More than 400 chemical compounds, including more than 60 cannabinoid compounds, can be extracted from the *Cannabis sativa* plant.[3] THC, cannabinol, cannabidiol, and cannabigerol are present in the largest quantities. All plant-derived cannabinoids (**phytocannabinoids**) share a similar chemical structure and physical and chemical properties. For example, they are highly lipid soluble and are poorly soluble in water. THC is 6,000 times more soluble in oil than water. THC's chemical name—Δ^9-tetrahydrocannabinol (Δ^9-THC)—and formula allow chemists and other life scientists to distinguish this molecule from its relatives: the "delta 9" refers to the fixed double bond between two carbon atoms (carbon #9 and #10, positioned adjacent to each other in one of the molecule's three carbon rings).[4]

In addition to the phytocannabinoids, there are two other groups of cannabinoids: **endocannabinoids**, which are naturally occurring or **endogenous cannabinoids** (meaning they are found in the human body), and chemically synthesized, or synthetic, cannabinoids. Unlike the phytocannabinoids, endogenous cannabinoids do not have a carbon ring chemical structure. Instead, they are long, unbranched, single chains of carbon atoms containing one or more double bonds. This chemical structure is similar to that of the nutritionally essential polyunsaturated **fatty acid**, known as arachidonic acid, from which the endocannabinoids are derived. The presence of double bonds makes a fatty acid "unsaturated," meaning it is not saturated with the maximum number of hydrogen atoms and is therefore less amenable to metabolic degradation to produce energy (i.e., burn calories).

Synthetic cannabinoids run the gamut. The first synthetic cannabinoid, dronabinol (trade name Marinol), was developed for medicinal purposes in the 1960s and approved by the U.S. Food and Drug Administration (FDA) as a prescription drug in 1985. Dronabinol has the same chemical formula and structure as THC found in smoked marijuana. Drug discovery and development efforts have produced synthetic agents similar in structure to phytocannabinoids and endocannabinoids, as well as others with unique chemical structures. Such research is geared toward designing new molecules by making minor changes in the chemical structure to yield desirable pharmacologic and biologic properties. However, even with the wealth of accumulated knowledge, sophisticated laboratory equipment, and artificial intelligence and modeling software, drug design is still largely a trial-by-error process primarily because of the difficulty in predicting specific action in such a highly complex systems like the human body.

CANNABINOID RECEPTORS

In the mid-1980s, biochemical and molecular studies provided conclusive evidence of the existence of cannabinoid receptors in the body. One key finding was the detection of specific receptors, or binding sites, by using a tagged **ligand** (a small molecule) consisting of a radioactively labeled synthetic cannabinoid, which had a high affinity for the cannabinoid receptor.[5]

In the early 1990s, two types of cannabinoid receptor were discovered and cloned: CB1 and CB2 (the 1 and 2 designations reflect the chronological order of their discovery). The differences between these two receptor types include their amino acid sequence, signaling pathways, tissue distribution, and sensitivity to drugs that bind to them.[6] The CB1 receptor is the major mediator of the psychoactive effects of THC and its derivatives, and many of the effects

THE BODY'S OWN THC:
ENDOGENOUS CANNABINOIDS

The discovery of cannabinoid binding sites in the brain in 1988 and the cloning of a cannabinoid receptor in 1990 suggested the existence of an endogenous cannabinoid that could bind to such receptors. Cannabinoid receptors and their endogenous cannabinoids together constitute the "endogenous cannabinoid system." The first endogenous cannabinoid identified—arachidonylethanolamide (anandamide, for short)—was isolated from brain tissue in 1992. Anandamide, whose name was derived from the Sanskrit word for bliss (*ananda*), is a small fatty acid produced by the brain that, like THC, binds to the CB1 and CB2 receptors. Another naturally occurring fatty acid with binding affinity for the CB1 and CB2 receptors, 2-arachidonoylglycerol (2-AG), was discovered in 1997. These two compounds are considered the main endogenous cannabinoids, producing effects similar to those of THC (e.g., appetite stimulation and pain reduction). One unexpected finding that emerged from THC research was the pivotal role of the endogenous cannabinoid system in so many physiological processes, including motor coordination, memory, control of appetite, pain modulation, and neuroprotection (prevention of brain injury and neurodegeneration from the effects of noxious stimuli such as toxins and hypoxia). Unlike classical **neurotransmitters** (the brain's chemical messengers) in the central and peripheral nervous systems, endogenous cannabinoids, which are also produced exclusively in the central and peripheral nervous system, are not stored in **synaptic vesicles** of neurons, but rather are produced "on demand." Endogenous cannabinoids exit the cell by either diffusion or via a carrier molecule and their action is terminated by uptake into cells and metabolic degradation.

R.G. Pertwee, "Cannabinoid Pharmacology: The First 66 Years," *British Journal of Pharmacology* 147, supplement 1 (January 2006): S163–S171; W.A. Devane, L. Hanus, A. Breuer, et al., "Isolation and Structure of a Brain Constituent that Binds to the Cannabinoid Receptor," *Science* 258, 5090 (18 December1992): 1946–1949; V. Di Marzo, "A Brief History of Cannabinoid and Endocannabinoid Pharmacology as Inspired by the Work of British Scientists," *Trends in Pharmacological Sciences* 27, 3 (March 2006): 134–140; C.C. Felder, E.M. Briley, J. Axelrod, et al. "Anandamide, an Endogenous Cannabimimetic Eicosanoid, Binds to the Cloned Human Cannabinoid Receptor and Stimulates Receptor-mediated Signal Transduction," *Proceedings of the National Academy of Sciences* 90, 16 (August 15, 1993): 7656–7660.

of the endogenous cannabinoids as well. In addition to CB1 and CB2 receptors, additional cannabinoid targets have been identified, including non-CB1 non-CB2 receptors and the vanilloid receptor.[7] However, more research is needed to further characterize these novel receptors. Cannabinoid receptors are found on the surface of select cells, including **neurons**, **endothelial cells**, and immune system cells. Each receptor is coupled to a membrane protein whose shape changes on binding with the appropriate ligand. This morphologic change sets in motion a complex series of reactions, involving several biochemical pathways, culminating in a specific physiologic response.[8]

The distribution of CB1 receptors has helped to predict and understand the effects of cannabinoids. CB1 receptors are found in greatest density in the central nervous system, particularly in brain regions associated with the behavioral effects of cannabinoids—namely, the cerebral cortex, hippocampus, basal ganglia, amygdala, hypothalamus, brain stem, spinal cord, and cerebellum.[9] The distribution pattern in the cerebral cortex explains many of marijuana's effects: this region of the brain is responsible for higher cognitive function, such as learning, problem solving, and processing of sensory information. Other effects are similarly understood in the context of the functions of specific brain regions: the hippocampus is essential for memory formation; the basal ganglia for movement; the amygdala for emotion; the cerebellum controls balance, equilibrium, and coordination of body movements; the brain stem and spinal cord are involved in pain modulation (the brain stem also controls the vomiting reflex); and the hypothalamus is involved in appetite.

CB1 receptors are nearly completely absent from the respiratory centers of the brain stem, a finding consistent with the observation that an overdose of marijuana does not result in death due to depressed respiration. In addition to the central nervous system, CB1 receptors are also expressed in the **peripheral nervous system** (the sensory and motor nerves that carry signals into and out of the central nervous system, respectively), both on sensory nerve fibers and in the **autonomic nervous system** (the motor nerves of the peripheral nervous system that carry signals to smooth and cardiac muscles, and glands), and by some non-neuronal cells, including immune cells.[10]

CB2 receptors are found in various cells and tissues of the immune system; they are abundant in the spleen and tonsils and their density in these tissues, is comparable to that of the CB1 receptors in the central nervous system.[11] Activation of CB2 receptors by THC results in suppression of both types of immunity: **humoral** (antibody) and **cell-mediated** (B and T lymphocyte) immune responses. In animal models, THC reduces airway inflammation (e.g., a localized immune response caused by the influenza virus) and **atherosclerosis**, a chronic inflammatory disease that can lead to myocardial infarction and stroke. CB2 receptors are found on some neurons inside and outside of the brain, but their role is unknown.[12]

As mentioned above, the biological and/or behavioral effects of cannabinoids are mediated through CB receptors. Drugs that bind to a receptor and produce an effect (or response) are called **agonists**, whereas drugs that bind to a receptor and do not produce a response are called **antagonists**. Typically, the magnitude of a response produced by a drug is related to the amount of drug administered; increasing the dose produces a greater response until a maximal response is achieved. Drugs that can produce a maximal response are called full agonists. However, not all agonists can produce a maximal response; those that produce a less than maximal response are called partial agonists. The phytocannabinoids, THC and cannabinol, are partial agonists, whereas, the endocannabinoid 2-arachidonylglycerol is a full agonist. Also, cannabanoids differ in their ability to bind to CB1 and CB2 receptors. Those that bind more or less equally to both receptors are called nonselective, whereas those that bind more to one than the other receptor are called selective (i.e., CB1-selective or CB2-selective). Both THC and cannabinol are nonselective and bind to both receptors. By contrast, two of the endocannabinoids show receptor selectivity: Anandamide is a partial agonist at CB1 receptors and 2-arachidonylglycerol is a full agonist at CB2 rceptors. Agonists with selectivity for CB1 or CB2 receptors have been developed.[13]

CANNABINOID PHARMACOLOGY

Pharmacologic studies examine and characterize the actions of drugs **in vitro** (literally, "in glass," the test tube or petri dish) and **in vivo** (in a living organism). Prior to the study of drug action in the human body, pharmacologists and toxicologists conduct in vitro experiments and then, if warranted, animal experiments to describe the specific actions of a drug in a complex biological system. The in vivo studies must include specific tests to determine how a drug behaves in a compartment such as brain or liver, and drug action at high doses to identify toxic and lethal doses.

Mechanism of Action

The discovery of the mechanism of action of THC is the direct result of can-nabinoid research and advances in **receptor biology** in the 1990s. The three classes of cannabinoids all exert their effects by binding with and activating cannabinoid receptors that are found on the surface of cells in several tissues in the body. The receptor-ligand binding interaction and the resulting biochem-ical changes underlie the pharmacodynamic effects of the cannabinoids—i.e., measurable physiologic changes post-binding. In the laboratory, the bind-ing interaction between receptors and ligands can be pinpointed in time and the biochemical, molecular, and cellular effects characterized as changes over time. In the body, the measurement of physiologic changes before and after a drug is administered is described in the pharmacodynamic profile of a drug.[14]

Pharmacodynamics: How THC Acts on the Body

THC exerts its effects through binding to cannabinoid receptors and interfer-ence with neurotransmitter release. The distribution of cannabinoid receptors in brain and other tissues is responsible for the variety of physiological, psy-chomotor, and cognitive effects. THC produces alterations in motor function, perception, cognition, memory, learning, endocrine function, and immunity, and has other influences, some of which appear to be interrelated with other neural pathways.

Although the effects of marijuana have been known for more than 5,000 years, early pharmacological research in animals only began in the 1940s with the testing of either a purified extract from *C. sativa* or a single cannabinoid. These early studies revealed that THC induced **catalepsy** (immobilization) in mice, central excitation in rabbits and mice (including seizures), and blocked the corneal reflex in rabbits (indicating depression of the brain stem). As much as scientists were intent on discovering how a molecule from a plant could have such specific and diverse effects on the central nervous system, studies were limited to observation and data recording. Indeed, the underlying mechanism of action responsible for THC's observed effects was not elucidated until well after the isolation, purification, and synthesis of THC in 1964.[15]

Studies of the behavioral and cognitive effects of marijuana include a clinical trial of THC, administered intravenously, in healthy individuals with limited previous exposure to marijuana. Two THC doses, comparable to the THC content in marijuana joints, were tested. A dose-response effect was only observed for certain measures (e.g., increased tiredness, distractibility, and memory impairment with the higher dose). The effects associated with THC were transient and included schizophrenia-like symptoms—specifically, suspiciousness and paranoia, feelings of grandiosity, disordered and disorganized thought processes, and the inability to filter out irrelevant background stimuli such as air conditioner noise. Other behavioral effects included blunted affect (lack of emotional response), feelings of detachment, distorted perception of time and environment, altered body perception, guilt feelings, tension, uncooperativeness, poor attention, preoccupation, unusual thought content, feelings of unreality, panic, increased anxiety and tiredness, and decreased "calm and relaxed" feeling.[16]

THC and other phytocannabinoids, endogenous cannabinoids, and synthetic cannabinoids affect nearly every body system and produce numerous effects (Table 3.1). Often, stimulation of CB1 receptors on neurons decreases or inhibits neurotransmitter release, which can explain many of the pharmacological effects of the cannabinoids. For example, **tachycardia** (rapid heart rate) and dry mouth are mediated by THC's effects on the release and turnover of the neurotransmitter acetylcholine. Also, the antiemetic properties of cannabinoids are mediated by the inhibition of the activation of serotonin 5-HT3 receptors, and the therapeutic effects on movement and spastic disorders are due to interactions with gamma-aminobutyric acid (GABA), glutamine, and dopamine transmitter systems.[17]

Several of the effects of cannabinoids are being investigated for their therapeutic potential, and include analgesia, muscle relaxation, immunosuppression, anti-inflammation, antiallergenic effects, sedation, improvement of mood, stimulation of appetite, antiemesis, lowering of intraocular pressure, **bronchodilation**, and neuroprotection.

Pharmacokinetics: How THC Moves Through the Body

To have an effect, a drug must enter the circulation and reach its site of action in specific tissues. Routes of drug administration include oral, intravenous, intramuscular, subcutaneous (under the skin), transcutaneous or transdermal (through the skin), sublingual (under the tongue) and buccal (through the lining of the mouth), intracranial (through the cranium, into the brain), and inhalation. Following administration, a drug is sequentially processed on its journey through the body beginning with absorption, the passage from the site of administration into the blood. Once in circulation, a drug may encounter many biomolecules, including sticky plasma proteins like albumin, and

Table 3.1. Effects of Cannabinoids on Body Systems	
Body system (cannabinoid receptor)	**Physiological Effects**
Nervous system (CB1)	Analgesia, muscle relaxation, appetite stimulation, vomiting, antiemetic effects, enhanced creativity, disturbed memory, unsteady gait, ataxia, slurred speech, weakness, deterioration or amelioration of motor coordination, fatigue, euphoria, enhanced well-being, dysphoria, anxiety, reduction of anxiety, depersonalization, increased sensory perception, heightened sexual experience, hallucinations, altered time perception, sleep
Cardiovascular system (CB1, CB2)	Tachycardia, enhanced heart activity, increased output, increase in oxygen demand, vasodilation, orthostatic **hypotension**
Respiratory system (CB1)	Bronchodilation
Gastrointestinal system (CB1, CB2)	Decreased salivation and dry mouth, reduced bowel movements and delayed gastric emptying
Immune system (CB2)	Impaired humoral and cell-mediated immunity, anti-inflammatory and antiallergic effects
Endocrine system (CB1)	Influence on luteinizing hormone, follicle-stimulating hormone, testosterone, prolactin, somatotropin (growth hormone), thyroid-stimulating hormone, glucose metabolism, reduced sperm count and sperm motility, disturbed menstrual cycle, and suppressed ovulation

Source: Adapted from F. Grotenhermen, "The toxicology of cannabis and cannabis prohibition," Chemistry & Biodiversity *4, 8 (August 2007): 1744–1769; V. Di Marzo, "A brief history of cannabinoid and endocannabinoid pharmacology as inspired by the work of British scientists,"* Trends in Pharmacological Sciences *27, 3 (March 2006): 134–140.*

is processed or metabolized before reaching its target receptor. The route of drug administration and drug formulation are two factors that affect the rate and degree of drug absorption. Bioavailability, the amount of drug absorbed after administration, is discussed below after the following presentation on metabolism and distribution.[18]

Smoking is the preferred route of marijuana administration by many users and, most likely unbeknownst to them, it efficiently delivers THC from the lungs to the brain, resulting in a rapid onset of effects. For many marijuana smokers, the intense sense of pleasure felt almost immediately after THC exposure to the central nervous system reinforces its use. However, the dose taken when smoked can vary from person to person because of differences in factors such as the number of puffs taken, the duration and spacing of puffs, the hold time, and volume inhaled with each puff. These variables allow the dose to be adjusted to the desired degree of effect.[19]

Unlike smoked marijuana, THC taken orally (synthetic THC in pill form) is absorbed from the gastrointestinal tract into the intestinal circulation, where nearly all of the dose (about 90% to 95%) is absorbed because of its high lipid solubility. The intestinal circulation flows directly to the liver, where THC is rapidly metabolized into other chemical compounds, and only a small amount of the dose (about 10% to 20%) reaches the systemic circulation. (This metabolism through the liver is called "first-pass" metabolism, referring to the metabolism that occurs before the circulation reaches the heart, where the blood is oxygenated.) When smoked, THC, which is highly lipid soluble, readily crosses the alveolar membrane of the lungs into the blood of the pulmonary capillaries. From there it is delivered to the heart where it is pumped directly to the brain, bypassing the liver and first-pass metabolism.

Detection of THC in plasma is immediately accompanied by the onset of cannabinoid effects. With inhalation, the plasma concentration of THC is detectable in the blood within seconds and increases with each inhalation.[20]

On cessation of smoking, the plasma concentration of THC decreases rapidly due to its rapid distribution into tissues and metabolism in the liver. Again, it is the highly lipophilic nature of THC that facilitates the initial uptake of THC by highly vascularized tissues, such as the lung, heart, brain, and liver. In tissues with limited blood supplies, such as fat, THC accumulates more slowly as it is redistributed from the vascular compartment. With prolonged drug exposure, THC concentrates in fat and may be retained for extended periods of time.[21]

In studies of individuals who smoked marijuana cigarettes, the terminal half-life of THC in plasma was determined to be about 4.1 days. In contrast, many commonly used drugs have much shorter plasma half-lives: penicillin, 20.7 minutes; tetracycline, 3.5 hours; diazepam, 20 hours; digoxin, 2 days. This means that THC redistributes slowly out of the blood and that its effects are prolonged. In essence, the blood acts as a THC reservoir. Approximately 80% to 90% of THC is excreted from the body within 5 days, mostly as metabolites: more than 65% is excreted in the feces and approximately 20% eliminated in urine. This slow removal of drug from the body prolongs marijuana's duration of action.[22]

As mentioned above, THC in pill form taken by mouth has a relatively low bioavailability of only 20% due to the fact that it undergoes first-pass metabolism. However, the bioavailability of THC in smoked marijuana ranges from 18% to 50% due to the variation in smoking technique between individuals.[23] Increased bioavailability leads to increased plasma THC concentration, which translates to a greater response (i.e., stronger drug effect). The binding of drugs to proteins in the blood (of which there are several kinds, the most notable being albumin) reduces the amount of "free" or "unbound" drug available for distribution, metabolism, and excretion. Only "free" drug can reach its target receptor. Plasma protein binding does not prevent a drug from reaching its site of action; it only slows the process. THC is highly bound to plasma proteins, a factor that contributes to its slow redistribution from the blood into the tissues.[24]

Like all drugs (and food and beverages), THC is metabolized, or chemically changed, in the body by enzymes into metabolites. But unlike food and beverages, drugs, environmental toxins, and plant products or herbal supplements are metabolized by unique enzymes. These enzymes, known as the **cytochrome P450** "superfamily" of enzymes, are found in almost all tissues of the body, but the highest levels are located in the liver. THC metabolism occurs mainly in the liver by specific enzymes of the cytochrome P450 complex (CYP 450 2C9, 2C19, and 3A4), which effectively decreases the amount of THC in the body. More than 100 THC metabolites have been identified. In addition to the liver, other tissues including the brain, intestines, and the lung contribute to the metabolism of cannabinoids, but to a much lesser extent.

Table 3.2. Drug Interactions Involving Cannabinoids	
Concomitant Drug	Clinical Effect
Amphetamines, cocaine, other sympathomimetic agents	Additive **hypertension**, tachycardia, possibly cardiotoxicity
Atropine, scopolamine, antihistamines, other anticholinergic agents	Additive or superadditive tachycardia, drowsiness
Amitriptyline, amoxapine, desipramine, other tricyclic antidepressants	Additive tachycardia, hypertension, drowsiness
Barbiturates, benzodiazepines, ethanol, lithium, opioids, buspirone, antihistamines, muscle relaxants, other central nervous system depressants	Additive drowsiness and central nervous system depression
Disulfiram	Reversible hypomanic reaction
Fluoxetine	Reversible hypomanic reaction
Antipyrine, barbiturates	Decreased clearance of these agents
Theophylline	Increased theophylline metabolism

Metabolism most often makes a drug inactive and accelerates its removal from the body.[25]

The activities of different cytochrome P450 enzymes vary and account for individual differences in the metabolism of the same drug. An asterisk and number designate a polymorphic variant. For example, CYP2C9*3 is one variant of CYP2C9 that is associated with a reduced enzymatic activity that may influence both the therapeutic and adverse effects of THC. After THC administration, individuals with the CYP2C9*3 variant have a higher level of THC and a lower level of the THC metabolite 11-nor-9-carboxy-9-tetrahydrocannabinol than individuals with the CYP2C9*1. This means that unaltered THC hangs around in the body longer and thus its effects are longer lasting in individuals with the CYP2C9*3 variant. Therefore, CYP2C9*3 carriers may be more easily sedated following administration of THC.[26]

Because drugs may use the same metabolic pathway, there is a potential for drug-drug interactions when THC is coadministered with a particular medication. Drug-drug interactions can also occur by the displacement of bound drugs from plasma proteins, resulting in the elevation of the displaced drug's concentration in the blood. Some interactions between THC and a coadministered medication can produce additive depressant or stimulant effects that may be potentially dangerous. Table 3.2 lists the potential drug interactions.

TRENDS IN CANNABINOID RESEARCH

Ongoing research is devoted to the biology, chemistry, and pharmacology of all classes of cannabinoids. Although advances in our understanding of cannabinoid drug action over the last 30 years have led to focused research projects with practical applications (e.g., THC-based medicines), there remain many gaps in our knowledge base. It has been suggested that modulating neurotransmitter release to maintain health is an important role of the neuronal CB1 component of the endocannabinoid system. Other recently discovered endogenous cannabinoids and additional CB receptors need to be further characterized to clearly identify their function and their potential relationship with other central nervous system pathways. To be sure, additional biomolecules involved in the endocannabinoid system have yet to be discovered, as do the genes that encode individual endocannabinoids, CB1 and CB2 receptors, and other cannabinoid-binding receptors. It is exciting times in the highly specialized research area of cannabinoid pharmacology; sooner or later the molecule(s) and mechanism controlling endocannabinoid production and release (the on/off switch) will be uncovered, and that discovery will be followed by another wave of innovative drug design efforts.

4
Use and Abuse

Sally, a high school sophomore, was excited but also a little apprehensive about her date with Jim, a popular junior with what seemed like a ton of friends. They were going to the homecoming football game and she knew that they'd be with some of his friends. At the football field, on the way to the stands, Jim was the perfect gentleman, introducing Sally to everyone they bumped into. Jim led Sally up to their seats and Sally started getting a sinking feeling when she realized that they'd be sitting up in one of the back row sections where everyone knew the potheads and druggies usually sat. Sally answered, "Sure," when Jim asked if the seats were okay. What else could she say? Sally was trying to follow the game, enjoy it even, but she was dreading the part when someone would light up. And then it happened. Sally thought the guy on her right was going to pass her a joint when Jim leaned over and said, "Sam is known for bogarting his joints, he doesn't share." Sally surprised herself with the words that came out of her mouth automatically: "Oh, I don't smoke." "I'm not smoking tonight either, or if I do, I won't inhale," Jim said to her with a grin. Then he took her hand and said, "Hope you can see through this haze. I usually slink down to the lower seats at halftime because I don't like missing any plays, plus that perfume lingers."

Rates of recreational use of marijuana in the United States are high, even in the global context. A rigorously conducted household survey carried out in 17 countries by the World Health Organization sampled a total of 85,052 persons with regard to lifetime marijuana use (on at least one occasion) and age at first use. For the period 2001–2004, lifetime marijuana use (on at least one occasion) was highest in the United States (42%), followed by New Zealand (41%). Among the seven European countries surveyed, the highest use was in

WORDS OF ABUSE

Addiction is a set of behaviors characterized by impaired control over drug use, **cravings**, continued use despite harm, compulsive use of a drug, and compulsion to obtain more of the drug for personal use.

Craving is the intense desire for a rewarding object or experience.

Dependence on a drug can be physical or biological and/or psychological. Physical dependence is a disturbance of the body's natural balance (equilibrium or homeostatic mechanism) due to repeated or chronic exposure to a drug. The disturbance is clearly evident when the drug is abruptly stopped and symptoms of drug withdrawal develop, such as restlessness, flu symptoms, fever, chills, runny nose, and aches and pains. Physical dependence can develop in any individual exposed to a particular drug for a prolonged period. Psychological dependence, the intense craving or desire to repeatedly use a drug or obtain a drug because it produces a sense of improved well-being, is a component of addictive behavior.

Tolerance to a drug refers to the loss of effectiveness associated with a specific dose over time: after repeated or chronic use of a specific drug, an increase in dose is required to produce the same effect that a smaller dose produced originally. Like dependence, tolerance is a biological phenomenon that can develop in any individual exposed to a particular drug for a prolonged period.

Withdrawal describes how the body reacts to no longer having a specific substance in its system. Withdrawal symptoms emerge when use of a substance is abruptly stopped. The brain and the rest of the body must adapt to the drug's absence. The physiological symptoms of withdrawal are generally unique to the classes of drugs. For marijuana, withdrawal occurs for the first 14 days after stopping use and one or more of the following symptoms may develop: anxiety, chills, craving, decreased appetite and eating, irritability, negative mood, pain, and sleep disturbance.

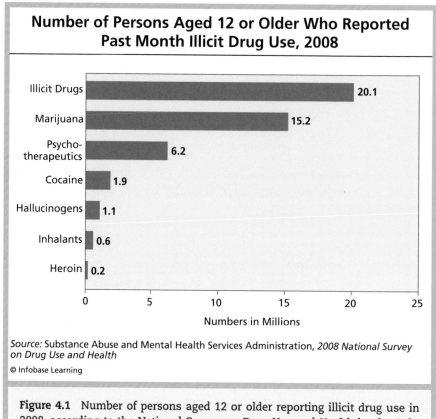

Number of Persons Aged 12 or Older Who Reported Past Month Illicit Drug Use, 2008

Illicit Drugs — 20.1
Marijuana — 15.2
Psycho-therapeutics — 6.2
Cocaine — 1.9
Hallucinogens — 1.1
Inhalants — 0.6
Heroin — 0.2

Numbers in Millions

Source: Substance Abuse and Mental Health Services Administration, *2008 National Survey on Drug Use and Health*

© Infobase Learning

Figure 4.1 Number of persons aged 12 or older reporting illicit drug use in 2008, according to the National Survey on Drug Use and Health by the Substance Abuse and Mental Health Services Administration.

the Netherlands (19.8%) and France (19.0%); the People's Republic of China had the lowest reported incidence at 0.3%. The median age for all surveyed countries was 18 to 19 years, with the exception of outlier countries: Nigeria and Israel (both 22 years of age) and Lebanon (21 years of age).[1]

Data analyses from survey research on substance use and abuse in the United States informs medical and social health professionals, public health officials, and policy makers. This chapter discusses two major surveys: the *National Survey on Drug Use and Health,* an annual report prepared from interviews of approximately 67,500 persons, and the *Monitoring the Future* survey, based on interviews of approximately 46,097 students from public and private schools.[2]

Although the goals and approaches of these two ambitious surveys are different (including sampling and data collection methods, questionnaires, and estimation methods), making comparisons between them difficult, comparisons between the surveys reveal that the rates of substance use reported in the *National Survey on Drug Use and Health* are lower than those reported in *Monitoring the Future*. The lower rates may be due to more underreporting in the household setting used in the *National Survey on Drug Use and Health* as compared with the school setting used in *Monitoring the Future*. Also, *Monitoring the Future* does not survey dropouts, a group that *National Survey on Drug Use and Health* has shown to have higher rates of illicit drug use.

TRENDS IN MARIJUANA USE

According to the 2008 *National Survey on Drug Use and Health,* marijuana was the most commonly used illicit drug among persons aged 12 or older. In the month prior to the survey interview, an estimated 15.2 million persons used marijuana (see Figure 4.1).

Of those using illicit drugs in 2008, just over one half (57.3%) reported that marijuana was the only drug used, whereas 75.7% reported having used marijuana in addition to other drugs. See Table 4.1 for illicit drug use by age group.

Among youths, marijuana use in the past month varied by age subgroup; marijuana was the most commonly used illicit drug in those 16 or 17 years old (12.7%) and 14 or 15 years old (5.7%). In those aged 12 or 13,

Table 4.1. Illicit Drug and Marijuana Use in 2008		
Age Group (years)	Illicit Dug Use (%)	Marijuana Use (%)
12 to 17	9.3	6.7
18 to 25	19.6	16.5
26 or older	5.9	4.2

Source: Substance Abuse and Mental Health Services Administration. Results from the 2008 National Survey on Drug Use and Health: National Findings.

marijuana was *not* the most commonly used illicit drug: 1.5% used prescription-type drugs nonmedically, 1.2% used inhalants, and 1.0% used marijuana.[3]

THE LINGO AND PARAPHERNALIA OF MARIJUANA USE

Like every subculture, the community of marijuana users has developed its own colorful language (lingo). Marijuana has more than 100 street names and is most commonly smoked in rolled cigarettes (called "joints"), in pipes, bongs, or in hollowed-out cigars (called "blunts" or "B"). A blunt that is consumed together with a 40-ounce bottle of malt liquor is called a "B-40." Marijuana is sometimes combined with another drug, such as crack cocaine, a combination known by various names, such as "primos" or "woolies." Joints and blunts sometimes are dipped in phencyclidine (PCP) and are called "happy sticks," "wicky sticks," "love boat," "dust," or "wets." Catching a "buzz" refers to a low level of intoxication producing an altered state of consciousness—best described as a calm, enjoyable, floaty feeling—after taking only two or three inhales ("hits" or "tokes"). "Stoned" refers to a high level of intoxication producing more intense effects.

"Head shops" entered the world of commerce in the heyday of marijuana's popularity in 1960s and 1970s, offering for sale numerous drug paraphernalia items. *Paraphernalia* refers to any equipment that is used to produce, conceal, or consume illicit drugs, which for marijuana includes pipes, bongs or water pipes (pipelike smoking devices with a long, tubular chamber, the bottom of which is filled with water through which inhaled smoke is filtered and cooled), vaporizers (a device used to heat marijuana to a temperature where the psychoactive cannabinoids evaporate without causing combustion, thus avoiding inhalation of harmful smoke toxins), and roach clips (used to hold the butt of a joint).

According to the U.S. Department of Justice, the federal drug paraphernalia statute, which falls under the Controlled Substances Act of 1970, makes it illegal to possess, sell, transport, import, or export drug paraphernalia.

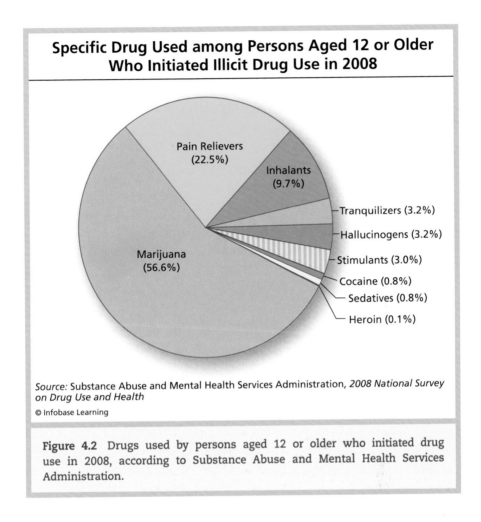

Specific Drug Used among Persons Aged 12 or Older Who Initiated Illicit Drug Use in 2008

Pain Relievers (22.5%)

Inhalants (9.7%)

Tranquilizers (3.2%)

Hallucinogens (3.2%)

Marijuana (56.6%)

Stimulants (3.0%)

Cocaine (0.8%)

Sedatives (0.8%)

Heroin (0.1%)

Source: Substance Abuse and Mental Health Services Administration, *2008 National Survey on Drug Use and Health*

© Infobase Learning

Figure 4.2 Drugs used by persons aged 12 or older who initiated drug use in 2008, according to Substance Abuse and Mental Health Services Administration.

Of the estimated 2.9 million persons aged 12 or older who used an illicit drug for the first time in 2008, the majority (56.6%, or 1.64 million persons) reported marijuana as the drug they tried for the first time (see Figure 4.2). The average age of recent first-time users, aged 12 to 49, was 17.8 years.[4]

Factors such as perceived risk of substance abuse, parental feelings about substance use, perceived availability, exposure to substance use prevention messages and/or programs, and religious beliefs can influence whether youths will use illicit drugs, including marijuana. One key factor is the perception of risk (i.e., how harmful the drug is to them). Among youths aged 12 to 17, 33.9% and 53.1% believed that there is "great risk" in smoking marijuana once a month and once or twice a week, respectively. Also, youths who believed their parents would "strongly disapprove" of their using marijuana (trying marijuana or hashish once or twice), which was most of this group (90.8%), reported less use (4.3%) than those who believed their parents would somewhat disapprove or neither approve nor disapprove (29.8%).

Overall, 46,097 students from 389 public and private schools in the 8th, 10th, and 12th grades participated in the 2009 *Monitoring the Future* survey. According to the 2009 results, marijuana use is increasing while the use of other illicit drugs is declining. Marijuana use in the previous 12 months (the annual prevalence rate) was 11.8% for 8th graders, 26.7% for 10th graders, and 32.8% for 12th graders. The proportions of those students saying they used any illicit drug in the past year were 15%, 29%, and 37%, respectively. Marijuana use among adolescents has been increasing gradually over the past two years, and over the past three years among 12th graders. In contrast, the use of any illicit drug other than marijuana has continued to decline for students in the 8th and 12th grades in 2009. The prevalence rates for using any drug other than marijuana in the prior 12 months are 7%, 12%, and 17% in grades 8, 10, and 12, respectively. Additionally, the 2008 survey revealed that the perceived risk of regular marijuana use decreased among 8th and 10th graders: 44.8% of 8th graders viewed occasional marijuana smoking as potentially harmful compared to 48.1% in the 2008 survey.[5]

In 2008, marijuana was the most widely used illicit drug: the frequency of its use varied by grade level (see Table 4.2). For example, among 8th-grade students, marijuana has been used at least once by 14.6% (1 in 7 students), with 10.9% reporting use in the prior year, and 5.8% in the prior month. The use of marijuana on a daily basis (defined as use on 20 or more occasions in the past 30 days) is noteworthy with 5.4% of 12th graders (1 in 19 students), 2.7% of 10th graders (1 in 37 students), and 0.9% of 8th graders (1 in 111 students) reporting daily marijuana use in the month prior to the survey.

Marijuana was the most frequently used illicit drug with 4%, 11%, and 18% of 8th, 10th, and 12th graders respectively reporting use on 20 or more occasions in their lifetime. Marijuana has surpassed alcohol as the most

Table 4.2. Percent of students reporting marijuana use in 2008			
Use	8th grade	10th grade	12th grade
Daily	0.9	2.7	5.4
Past month	5.8	13.8	19.4
Past Year	10.9	23.9	32.4
Lifetime	14.6	29.9	42.6

Lifetime = Used one or more times in their life
Past year = Used one or more times in the past year
Past month = Used one or more times in the past month
Daily = Used 20 or more times in the past 30 days
Source: L.D. Johnston, P.M. O'Malley, J.G. Bachman, and J.E. Schulenberg, Monitoring the Future National Survey Results on Drug Use, 1975–2008: Volume I, Secondary School Students (adapted from Table 4.2, p104), http://monitoringthefuture.org/pubs.html.

frequently used drug across all of these grade levels. The rates for daily alcohol use in 2008 were 0.7%, 1.0%, and 2.8% in grades 8, 10, and 12, respectively. About 75% of 12th grade marijuana users said they usually get moderately or very high.

The relationship between marijuana use in the past year and demographic information, such as gender, college plans, socioeconomic status, and race, for 8th, 10th, and 12th graders is provided in Table 4.3.

As shown in Table 4.3, the proportion of students that used marijuana once or more (in 2008) increased by grade level: 12th grade white students had the highest use. A gender difference was noted in marijuana use (males > females) across all grade levels, and college plans are related to use; annual marijuana use is reported by 30.2% of the college-bound 12th graders versus 41.0% of the non-college-bound 12th graders with similar findings for 8th and 10th graders. There was no appreciable effect of population density on marijuana use. Regional use in the Northeast was highest in 12th grade and lowest in 8th grade, and little variation at 10th grade. Socioeconomic status (as measured by average education attainment level of the student's parents) was inversely related to marijuana use in 8th and 10th graders, but was not associated with use in 12th graders. Marijuana use varied by race and by grade level with Hispanic students having the highest rate in 8th grade,

Table 4.3. Annual Marijuana Use by Grade in 2008 (values are in percent except where noted)			
	8th grade	10th grade	12th grade
Total number of students interviewed	15,700	15,100	14,000
Respondents using in the past year	10.9	23.9	32.4
Gender:			
Male	12.2	25.5	35.1
Female	9.5	22.2	29.5
College plans:			
None or less than 4 years	27.7	43.5	41.0
Complete 4 years	9.4	21.4	30.2
Region where school is located:			
Northeast	8.3	26.3	36.6
Midwest	12.6	22.6	31.1
South	11.5	24.0	31.0
West	10.3	23.4	32.8
Population density of area where school is located:			
Large metropolitan statistical area	9.9	24.2	34.8
Other metropolitan statistical area	11.8	24.7	31.2
Non- metropolitan statistical area	10.4	21.7	32.2
Parental education (average of mother's and father's highest level completed)			
did not graduate high school	18.5	30.2	30.5
high-school graduate	14.6	28.3	32.8
some college	11.8	26.0	32.0
college graduate	8.2	19.8	32.7
graduate or professional school	6.7	18.9	32.8
Race:			
White	9.6	24.6	33.9
African-American	10.6	20.6	26.8
Hispanic	13.2	26.6	27.3

Source: Monitoring the Future National Survey Results on Drug Use, 1975–2008. Adapted from *Tables D-7, D-8,* and *D-9.*

white students the lowest rate in 8th grade but the highest in 12th grade, and African-American students having the lowest rates in 10th and 12th grades.

While marijuana is the most frequently used of all the illicit drugs, it has one of the lowest levels of perceived harmfulness (risk) and disapproval. Slightly more than half (52%) of all 12th graders think that regular use of marijuana involves a great risk, only 17% view experimenting with marijuana—trying marijuana once or twice—involves great risk, and 26% see great risk in occasional use. In contrast, younger students, particularly 8th graders, are somewhat more likely than 12th graders to see marijuana use as dangerous. For example, in 2008, about twice as many 8th graders (48%) as 12th graders (26%) see occasional marijuana use as involving great risk. Among 12th graders, the rate of disapproval of marijuana varies widely for different levels of usage; more than half (56%) disapprove of trying marijuana once or twice, more than two thirds (67%) disapprove of its occasional use, and 80% disapprove of regular use. In contrast to 12th graders, 65% of 10th graders and 77% of 8th graders disapprove of trying marijuana once or twice. A similar pattern was seen in 8th and 10th graders' disapproval of occasional and regular marijuana use compared with the disapproval among 12th graders; the lower the grade, the higher the rate of disapproval. After alcohol, the drug students are exposed to most frequently is marijuana. Seventy percent of 12th graders reported having been around people who used marijuana during the prior year. Some (27%) said they have often been around people using it to get high, and another 23% said they have been exposed occasionally. Twenty percent said that most or all of their friends smoke marijuana, and 78% said that they have at least some friends who use the drug. Both 10th-grade and 8th grade students are less likely than 12th graders to have friends who use marijuana: 38% of 8th graders and 65% of 10th graders said they have friends who use marijuana.

TRENDS IN DRUG ABUSE

The *2008 National Survey on Drug Use and Health* revealed that 7 million persons aged 12 and older were dependent on or abused illicit drugs in 2008. Of these, 4.2 million were dependent on or abused marijuana or

(*continues on page 60*)

K2: A LEGAL HIGH

According to news articles in early 2010, folks are clamoring about K2. Not the second highest mountain in the world (located on the border between China and Pakistan), but the herbal product. Although sold as incense and despite the warning "not for consumption" on the package, the product is rolled into a cigarette or smoked in a pipe and produces a high similar to that achieved with smoked cannabis. In addition to herbs and spices, K2 contains a synthetic form of THC, called JWH-018, which is likely responsible for psychoactive effects reportedly similar to those of THC. The abbreviation JWH is the initials of the organic chemist, John W. Huffman, who first synthesized the compound in 1995. Like THC, JWH-018 binds to both CB1 and CB2 receptors. But JWH-018 is a more potent agonist of CB1 receptors than is THC; also, JWH-018 is a full agonist (it can produce a maximal effect) whereas THC is a partial agonist (it produces less-than-maximal effect) through binding to these receptors.

K2 is just one of many other similar herbal products that are sold under different names such as "Spice," "Spice Gold," "Sence," "Chill X," "Smoke," and "Genie." Often these products contain JWH-018 as well as other cannabinoids in different amounts or combinations to produce cannabis-like psychoactive effects. Although these herbal products are considered "legal highs" at the present time, the psychoactive ingredients they contain are not listed on the package label. The recognition that the active ingredients are synthetic cannabinoids may change their status in the United States from legal to illegal, as many European countries have done already, and as state legislatures around the country are beginning to do.

Its U.S. media coverage may be growing, but it appears that K2 and other similar herbal products may have been available since 2004, primarily through sale on the Internet and in "head shops." Surprisingly, it was not until December 2008, when several laboratories in Europe reported that two synthetic cannabinoids—JWH-018 and CP-47-497—were found in samples of "Spice," that the active ingredients in the product were revealed. In 2009, another potent synthetic cannabinoid, HU-210, was found in "Spice" products seized by the U.S. Drug Enforcement Administration. So far, at least nine synthetic cannabinoids have been found in "Spice" and similar products, but there are more than 100 known synthetic compounds with cannabinoid receptor activity.

The synthetic cannabinoids found in K2 and other herbal products have been tested only in the laboratory (in vitro or in animals), and there have been no studies in humans, so little is known about their metabolism and toxicology. As a result, the potential health risks associated with their use are unknown. However, a case study published in the medical literature in 2009 of a 20-year-old man who smoked "Spice Gold" daily for eight months described physical withdrawal and dependence associated with its use. In addition, accidental overdose with a risk of severe psychiatric complications may be more likely to occur because the type and amount of cannabinoid

(continues)

Figure 4.3.   K2, a mixture of dried plant matter and synthetic cannabinoids.   (© *AP Images*)

(*continued*)

may vary considerably from batch to batch even within the same product. The widespread availability of smokable herbal products laced with synthetic cannabinoids is a significant new development in the field of "designer drugs."

European Monitoring Centre for Drugs and Drug Addiction, "Thematic Paper—Understanding the 'Spice' Phenomenon," 2009, http://www.emcdda.europa.eu (accessed February 22, 2010); J.W. Huffman et al., "Variation of the Alkyl Side Chain in Delta 8-THC," *Life Science* 56, 23–24 (1995): 2021–2024; U.S. Zimmermann et al., "Withdrawal Phenomena and Dependence Syndrome After the Consumption of 'Spice Gold.'" *Deutsch Aerzteblatt International* 106, 27 (2009): 464–467; U.S. Drug Enforcement Agency, "'Spice'—Plant Material(s) Laced with Synthetic Cannabinoids or Cannabinoid Mimicking Compounds," Microgram Bulletin March 2009, http://www.justice.gov/dea/programs/forensicsci/microgram/mg0309/mg0309.html (accessed February 22, 2010).

(*continued from page 57*)

hashish (representing 1.7% of the total population aged 12 or older, and 60.1% of all those classified with illicit drug dependence or abuse). Compared with other illicit drugs, marijuana had the highest rate of past year dependence or abuse followed by prescription pain relievers and cocaine (see Figure 4.4).[6]

The rate of substance dependence or abuse was about twofold greater in males (11.5%) aged 12 and older compared with females (6.4%). However, among youths aged 12 to 17, the rate of substance dependence or abuse was lower for males (7.0%) than females (8.2%).

In 2008, the drugs for which most recent treatment was received in the past year among persons aged 12 and older was alcohol (2.6 million persons), marijuana (947,000 persons), cocaine (663,000 persons), pain relievers (601,000 persons), heroin (341,000 persons), stimulants (336,000 persons), tranquilizers (326,000 persons), and hallucinogens (287,000 persons). Treatment received could be at sites such as a hospital (inpatient), rehabilitation facility (outpatient or inpatient), mental health center, emergency room, private doctor's office, prison or jail, or a self-help group, such as Alcoholics Anonymous

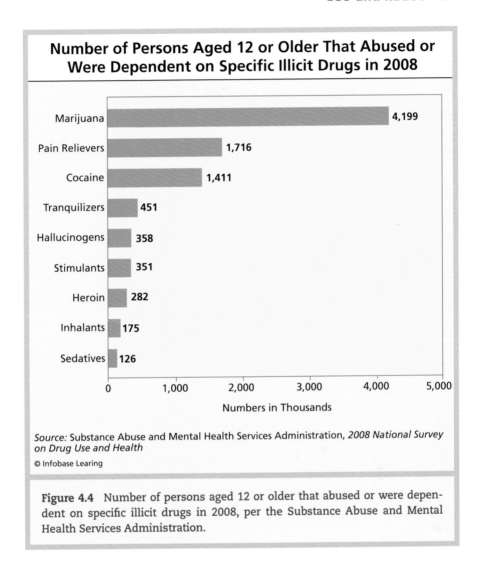

Number of Persons Aged 12 or Older That Abused or Were Dependent on Specific Illicit Drugs in 2008

- Marijuana: 4,199
- Pain Relievers: 1,716
- Cocaine: 1,411
- Tranquilizers: 451
- Hallucinogens: 358
- Stimulants: 351
- Heroin: 282
- Inhalants: 175
- Sedatives: 126

Numbers in Thousands

Source: Substance Abuse and Mental Health Services Administration, *2008 National Survey on Drug Use and Health*

© Infobase Learing

Figure 4.4 Number of persons aged 12 or older that abused or were dependent on specific illicit drugs in 2008, per the Substance Abuse and Mental Health Services Administration.

or Narcotics Anonymous. More than one site could be reported for receiving treatment.

Another source of data on drug abuse is the "Treatment Episode Data Set" of the Substance Abuse and Mental Health Services Administration, which provides information on admissions to substance abuse treatment services in the United States. According to this data set, 1.8 million admissions were reported for substance abuse treatment in 2007. Of these, marijuana accounted for 16%, or 287,933 admissions. Alcohol and opiate use led admissions for substance abuse treatment accounting for 40% and 19% of admissions, respectively. The database does not include all admissions to substance abuse treatment but mainly facilities that are licensed or certified by the state substance abuse agency to provide substance abuse treatment, such as those that receive state alcohol and/or drug agency funds.[7]

5
Marijuana Addiction Treatment

Ken reluctantly agreed to enter the outpatient program of a drug treatment facility so that he wouldn't miss any more school than he already had. Ken had been lying to his parents and school administrators, insisting that he quit using marijuana. His parents were initially stunned when they were summoned by Ken's school to discuss his grades, his attitude, his behavior, and even his dress and hygiene. They assumed that Ken's his new clique of friends and his partying were attributable to senioritis. Ken had hid and lied about his first quarter report card, and only at the conference did his parents learn that he was failing three courses. As a high school senior, Ken got early notice of acceptance into his first choice for college provided he maintain his grade point average for both semesters of his senior year. Ken was a stellar student in his freshman, sophomore, and junior years, but he began skipping classes and then entire days right from the start of his senior year.

Ken promised to stop smoking pot, saying that it was no big deal, that he didn't need any help. The school counselor advised Ken's parents to support Ken, but not to accept all of his answers, especially when they're contradictory or don't make sense. Armed with information about marijuana's effects, Ken's parents would confront him at home when he was being uncharacteristically talkative, laughing inappropriately, and saying things like, "I guess you had to be there because it was hilarious," and walking away. Ken said he was smoking cigarettes instead of marijuana, and that they should be glad. Ken's grades were

63

improving and some of his old friends seemed to be back in his life, although not like before. Then Ken got into a "fender-bender" and after giving an unsatisfactory explanation and not taking responsibility, Ken was handed an ultimatum from his parents.

Ken and his parents had to sign a contract with the therapist and case worker at the drug facility, saying that they were all committed to attending family counseling, that Ken would go to individual and peer counseling sessions twice a week to help Ken break his pattern of so-called occasional marijuana use. Ken and his parents agreed that total abstinence without medical treatment was a realizable goal. Ken agreed to the program's terms to be tested for cannabinoids at every visit to monitor his marijuana use. His answers to the program's question-naire would be corroborated with findings from laboratory analyses of one of several testing methodologies to detect THC: urinalysis, sweat patch, or hair specimen. The sensitivities of the assays vary. The one that measures THC concentrations in hair is sensitive enough to allow distinction between daily and non-daily users.

Each year, approximately 20,000 to 30,000 new marijuana users in the United States develop drug dependency within the first two years of beginning smok-ing marijuana. That statistic is equivalent to 1% to 2% of all new marijuana smokers. According to the *2008 National Survey on Drug Use and Health*, an annual household survey sponsored by the U.S. Substance Abuse and Men-tal Health Services Administration that interviews approximately 67,500 U.S. civilian residents each year, of all illicit drugs, marijuana had the highest rate of past year dependence or abuse in 2008, followed by pain relievers and cocaine. Trending data for the rate of marijuana abuse or dependence among those 12 years of age and older during the last six-year period for which the latest figures are available (2002 to 2008) show no significant change: 4.3 mil-lion users in 2002 versus 4.2 million in 2008. The rate for 2008 was higher than that for 2007: 4.2 million versus 3.9 million, respectively.[1]

Drug dependence has a biological component in which the body's equi-librium is disturbed after repeated or chronic exposure to a particular drug to such a degree that physical symptoms develop after abrupt withdrawal of the drug. Withdrawal symptoms from marijuana include chills, muscle pain, decreased appetite and food intake, disturbed sleep, and craving. The

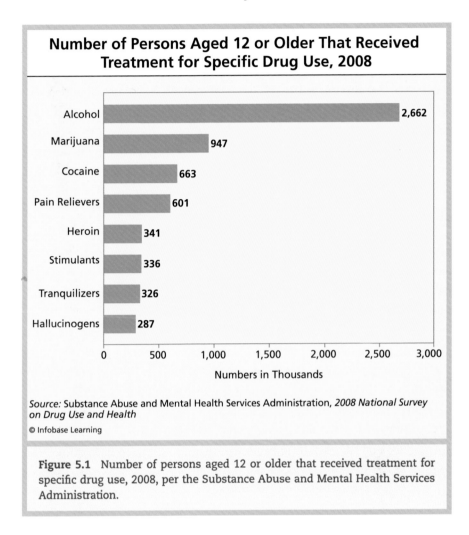

Number of Persons Aged 12 or Older That Received Treatment for Specific Drug Use, 2008

Drug	Numbers in Thousands
Alcohol	2,662
Marijuana	947
Cocaine	663
Pain Relievers	601
Heroin	341
Stimulants	336
Tranquilizers	326
Hallucinogens	287

Numbers in Thousands

Source: Substance Abuse and Mental Health Services Administration, *2008 National Survey on Drug Use and Health*

© Infobase Learning

Figure 5.1 Number of persons aged 12 or older that received treatment for specific drug use, 2008, per the Substance Abuse and Mental Health Services Administration.

psychological component of drug dependence, defined as an intense craving or desire to repeatedly use a drug or obtain a drug because it produces a feeling of improved well-being, is a component of addictive behavior. Addiction to marijuana, like that for other substances of abuse, has genetic, psychosocial, and environmental influences, and is characterized by impaired control over drug use or compulsive drug use, continued drug use despite harm to self and others, and cravings.[2] An addict may not fully comprehend the totality of harm caused by their drug-using and drug-seeking behaviors, and they may not agree that they need to stop using.[3]

Treatment for marijuana addiction was largely ignored until the 1990s primarily because dependency with prolonged use had not been documented. It is now known that abrupt cessation of marijuana use results in withdrawal symptoms that disappear if drug use is resumed—the classic definition of drug dependency. Furthermore, this phenomenon occurs in all animal species tested in the laboratory setting.[4] Nevertheless, the need for marijuana addiction treatment is not uniformly recognized throughout the health care profession, and treatment is considered unnecessary or is given a slight nod with mild recommendations: "for patients experiencing significant discomfort, treatment is supportive."[5]

Data from drug addiction treatment programs provide proof that marijuana addiction does exist. According to the Treatment Episode Data Set, a national database of admissions data from detoxification and rehabilitation facilities that treat alcohol and drug abuse, from the Substance Abuse and Mental Health Services Administration, for the year 2007, marijuana dependence was the third most common reason for admission to a drug treatment program (behind alcohol and opiate dependence). Data analyses also show that marijuana dependence has increased during the 10-year period from 1997 to 2007, although it has remained flat for the last four years: the proportion of admissions to treatment facilities for marijuana abuse increased from 12% in 1997 to 16% in 2003 through 2007.[6] Findings from the *2008 National Survey on Drug Use and Health* revealed that an estimated 947,000 persons aged 12 and older reported receiving treatment for marijuana use in 2008.[7]

TREATMENT APPROACHES

Psychotherapy and pharmacotherapy are the two treatment options for marijuana dependence, although at this time, pharmacologic approaches are experimental.[8] The most common psychotherapeutic, or behavioral, intervention approaches for the management of marijuana dependence are similar to those shown to be effective in treating alcohol dependence.[9] These approaches include cognitive behavioral therapy, motivational enhancement, and motivational incentives, and can be provided on an outpatient basis, meaning that hospitalization or treatment facility admission is not required.[10] Compared with cocaine and other drugs of abuse known to have a high risk of dependency, marijuana consistently scores lower on scales that measure drug effects and impairment.[11] This fact does not minimize the degree or nature of marijuana use–related problems; rather, it highlights the challenges facing therapists and drug abuse treatment providers to successfully treat marijuana addiction. Like other drugs of abuse, total abstinence from marijuana use after treatment is difficult to achieve and relapse rates are high. For this reason, pharmacologic intervention with medications is warranted and several targets have been identified: the CB1 cannabinoid receptor; endocannabinoids and their metabolites and related enzymes; signaling molecules of the endocannabinoid system and those involved in relevant pathways in the brain, such as the reward pathway.

Behavioral Interventions

For marijuana dependence, cognitive behavioral therapy is typically given as weekly individual or group sessions. These therapy sessions teach the coping skills needed to quit marijuana use and work on developing strategies to avoid, ignore, or cope with cues or triggers that could lead to marijuana use. Problem-solving skills, drug-refusal skills, and general lifestyle management skills are developed and strengthened. The sessions also examine recent marijuana use or cravings and interactive exercises, such as role-playing, are employed to build and reinforce drug avoidance and drug abstinence behaviors.

Another behavioral approach to marijuana addiction treatment is motivational enhancement, which is typically provided in individual sessions. In this intervention, therapists work with patients to strengthen the commitment to quit marijuana use and to increase patients' motivation to change (to stop smoking marijuana). The pros and cons of marijuana use are explored with the individual, and the belief in one's ability to succeed in quitting is affirmed. The use of motivational incentives with prizes or vouchers for abstaining from marijuana is another behavioral treatment approach.

Several clinical trials have been conducted to evaluate the effectiveness of these behavioral interventions in promoting and achieving cessation of marijuana use. In adults, randomized controlled trials have shown that the combined use of cognitive behavioral therapy and motivational enhancement is more effective than motivational enhancement alone: combined methods lead to greater long-term abstinence rates and greater reduction in the frequency of marijuana use. However, at the present time, the most effective behavioral treatment for marijuana dependence appears to be the use

Figure 5.2 Therapy is one treatment option available to those addicted to marijuana. *(National Institute of Mental Health)*

of abstinence-based voucher programs in combination with cognitive behavioral therapy and motivational enhancement. Abstinence-based voucher programs employ the use of vouchers with a monetary value that increases with each consecutive negative drug test, thus providing an incentive to abstain from marijuana use. Such a combination treatment approach that includes all three modalities yields positive results in adults and adolescents.[12]

Other non-pharmacologic interventions continue to be evaluated in specific patient populations in different settings. For example, one randomized controlled trial that looked to test the success of different interventions in adolescents 14 to 18 years of age included a substance-use monitoring contract between the parent and adolescent and a parent-training program, in addition to the threesome of abstinence-based vouchers, cognitive behavioral therapy, and motivational enhancement. Compared with those receiving cognitive behavioral therapy and motivational enhancement only, adolescents in the experimental treatment armed with the substance-use monitoring contract had increased abstinence rates that were maintained post-treatment: 50% abstained from marijuana use for 10 or more weeks after treatment, compared with 18% of the "control group" (no substance-use monitoring contract).[13]

Borrowing from the playbook of alcohol dependency treatment, a study investigated the effectiveness of screening and brief intervention in a pediatric emergency department of a busy urban hospital. Screening and brief intervention has been successful in changing alcohol abuse behaviors among emergency department patients. This 2006–2007 randomized pilot study screened patients aged 14 to 21 years who were included in the study if they used marijuana in the past month, but excluded patients who also had problems with alcohol abuse. Of the 7,084 patients screened, 325 were eligible (4.6%), and 210 were enrolled in the study and randomized to one of three treatment groups: an intervention group that received assessment of marijuana use, resource handouts, written advice about marijuana risks, 3- and 12-month follow-up appointments, and a 20-minute structured conversation conducted by older peers, plus a 10-day booster telephone call; a control group that received assessment of marijuana use, resource handouts, written advice, and 3- and 12-month follow-up appointments; and a second control group that received assessment of marijuana use, resource handouts, written advice, and a single 12-month follow-up appointment. For the intervention group, peer educators used a motivational interview technique adapted for adolescents to elicit daily life context and goals, provide feedback, discuss the pros and cons of marijuana use, assess readiness to change, evaluate strengths and assets, negotiate a contract for change, and make referrals to treatment and/or other resources. Not surprisingly, at the 12-month follow-up visit, abstinence from marijuana use in the previous 30 days was highest among patients in the intervention group; this group also had the greatest reduction in days using marijuana over the last 12 months. No significant difference in marijuana use was found between the two control groups.[14]

Pharmacologic Therapies

Because of the relatively recent elucidation of the endocannabinoid system, particularly with regard to the selectivity of specific cannabinoid compounds for the CB1 and CB2 cannabinoid receptors in the central nervous system, the

EXPLOITING A CANNABINOID RECEPTOR

Chronic or intermittent repeated use of drugs of abuse, including alcohol, nicotine, THC, and opiates, produce changes in the central nervous system that leads to physical drug dependence. All drugs of abuse activate a common endogenous neural pathway in the brain: the mesolimbic dopamine brain reward systems. CB1 receptors are found on cells in this reward pathway and, upon binding with an endogenous or exogenous ligand, can modulate the release of the neurotransmitter dopamine in an area of the brain called the nucleus accumbens. Nearly all drugs of abuse elevate dopamine levels in the nucleus accumbens. CB1 receptor antagonists, through their interaction with the CB1 receptors located in these reward pathways, are promising new medications for the treatment of drug dependence because they block the rewarding effects of a variety of classes of drugs. One example is the CB1 receptor antagonist, rimonabant (SR141716), a synthetic cannabinoid developed to treat obesity by the French pharmaceutical company Sanofi-Aventis, currently under investigation for the treatment of alcohol dependence and nicotine addiction. This drug has not been approved by the U.S. Food and Drug Administration. Other CB1 receptor antagonists with more favorable side effects profiles are being identified and tested.

B. Le Foll and S.R. Goldberg. "Cannabinoid CB1 Receptor Antagonists as Promising New Medications for Drug Dependence," *The Journal of Pharmacology and Experimental Therapeutics* 312 (2005): 875–883.

pharmacologic treatment for marijuana dependence and withdrawal is currently a hot research area. Ultimately, the research will translate to prescription medications of the kind available to treat addictions to other substances of abuse, such as heroin and cocaine. Findings from the intersecting fields of pharmacology, biochemistry, molecular biology, neuroscience, and psychiatry have already provided incredible insights into the mechanism underlying the development of marijuana dependence. Continual or prolonged exposure to marijuana leads to a dampening of CB1 receptor expression on cell surfaces (in essence, fewer receptors), altered binding affinities, and/or desensitization of receptor function, resulting in a decreased response, which in turn, is part of the addiction cycle—that is, the progressively decreasing response leads to the use of greater amounts or greater frequency of drug use.[15] Marijuana dependence also likely develops due to the interaction between the endocannabinoid system and other systems of the nervous system, such as the opioid system (involved in pain modulation) and the dopamine system (involved in mood). The molecular events that follow either stimulation or inhibition of the CB1 and/or CB2 receptor lead to modulation of neurotransmitter release in brain regions involved in the regulation of pain, emotion, motivation, and cognition.[16] Chronic marijuana use changes the brain circuitry, so to speak, such that dependence develops. Abrupt discontinuation of marijuana use among chronic users leads to the development of withdrawal symptoms, which contribute to relapse and the inability to achieve abstinence (i.e., withdrawal symptoms are alleviated if marijuana use is resumed). These observations, combined with insights gleaned from the molecular neuroscience of marijuana dependence, suggest that pharmacologic interventions can prevent relapse and reduce dependence. So-called cannabinoid replacement therapy, which uses a compound such as synthetic THC (dronabinol) that has been shown to be safe in humans and is already commercially available in capsule form, is one pharmacologic approach. Placebo-controlled clinical studies have in fact shown that oral THC administered during withdrawal at doses that did not produce intoxication significantly decreased anxiety, chills, craving, decreased eating, and sleep disturbance associated with marijuana abstinence.[17] Early results with the combination of oral THC and lofexidine, an alpha 2-receptor agonist used to treat hypertension, showed significantly reduced withdrawal symptoms and relapse beginning on the first day of marijuana abstinence.[18]

Other approaches include targeting the CB1 receptor through inhibition, e.g., CB1 receptor antagonists (see sidebar, "Exploiting a Cannabinoid Receptor"), and compounds that trigger increased levels of endocannabinoids through inhibition of metabolic enzymes. For example, the investigative agent URB597, an inhibitor of fatty-acid amide hydrolase, which is the enzyme responsible for the degradation of anandamide and another well-characterized endocannabinoid, has been shown to increase anandamide levels in brain tissue of laboratory animals.[19] At the physiologic level, administration of URB597 produces analgesic, antianxiety, and antidepressant effects in animal models. It should be pointed out that non-cannabinoid medications, such as the antidepressants buproprion and nefazodone, have been clinically evaluated to alleviate withdrawal symptoms without success: Treatment with these drugs led to worsening of irritability, anxiety, and depression.[20]

Ongoing efforts by the U.S. National Institutes of Health, in particular the National Institute on Drug Abuse, are in place to promote basic and clinical science research that identifies and evaluates safe and effective medications to treat marijuana addiction and/or the medical and psychiatric consequences of marijuana use (including the actual synthesis or development of candidate compounds). As clearly stated in a program announcement, the National Institute on Drug Abuse ". . . is encouraging research in this area because there is a high prevalence of marijuana use in the general population accompanied with an increasing misperception that its use poses low health risk, there is limited research in this area, and there are no effective pharmacological treatments available for these [addiction] disorders."[21]

6

Marijuana and the Law

Ben Curtis, a pitchman in Dell computer commercials from 2000–2003, was out walking in his Lower East Side Manhattan neighborhood late one Sunday night in 2003 looking to buy some pot. On the corner of Ludlow and Rivington streets, he met a man who sold him some. Unknown to the two men, their transaction was being observed by a special antinarcotics detail of the New York Police Department. When the officers saw the purchase going down, they moved in and arrested both men. Curtis had purchased less than 2 ounces of pot, and was charged with criminal possession of marijuana. Under New York State law, criminal possession—more than 25 grams (0.88 ounces) but less than 57 grams (2.01 ounces)—is a misdemeanor punishable by a maximum fine of $500 and maximum jail time of three months. After being held in custody overnight, Curtis was arraigned in Manhattan Criminal Court the next afternoon.

Manhattan Criminal Court Judge Ellen Coin adjourned the case for one year, stating that the charges could be dismissed if Curtis avoids trouble for the next 12 months. Because the amount of marijuana in Curtis's case was at the upper end of a misdemeanor possession charge, the judge could have sentenced Curtis to three months in jail and imposed a $500 fine. Fortunately for Curtis, he was released and the case adjourned in contemplation of dismissal (that's the legal language meaning that the case is expected to be dismissed and the offender's record expunged if he stays out of trouble for the next year). Because this was Curtis's first offense, there was another option. New York State *law has an "adjournment in contemplation for dismissal" procedure, which allowed Curtis to stay out of jail. He did not have to plead guilty to anything. He had to promise stay out of trouble for one year to have the charges against him dropped. His police fingerprint file and criminal record were destroyed.*

The early European settlers of this nation brought *C. sativa* seeds and plants with them in the 1600s, and by the 1800s the marijuana plant was a major crop because of its commercial value as fiber for rope and cloth. It was at about the early 1800s that marijuana was introduced into Western medicine for numerous ailments, and its use as a therapeutic drug rapidly spread. Soon after, its recreational use came into vogue. As the use of marijuana by society

DRUG SCHEDULES ESTABLISHED BY THE CONTROLLED SUBSTANCES ACT

Schedule I
- The drug or substance has a high potential for abuse.
- The drug or substance has no currently accepted medical use in the United States
- There is a lack of accepted safety for use of the drug or other substance under medical supervision.

Schedule II
- The drug or substance has a high potential for abuse.
- The drug or substance has a currently accepted medical use in the United States or has a currently accepted medical use with severe restrictions.
- Abuse of the drug or substance may lead to severe psychological or physical dependence.

Schedule III
- The drug or other substance has a lower potential for abuse than the drugs or substances in Schedules I and II.

evolved, so too have the laws regarding its use. Although the commercial cultivation in the United States has been discontinued since the Marijuana Tax Act of 1937, the laws concerning marijuana cultivation were based on economics (availability, supply, and need). By contrast, the laws regarding the recreational and medical use of marijuana are based on societal mores (e.g., moral values), medical issues, and politics. The laws regarding marijuana use have been and continue to be in a state of flux. [1]

One key law, passed by Congress in 1970, was the Controlled Substance Act, which sought to regulate or control the manufacture, importation, possession, use, and distribution of certain substances. The Controlled Substance Act created a list of substances that were classified according to "schedules" based on a substance's potential for abuse, safety or dependence, and medical

- The drug or substance has a currently accepted medical use in the United States.
- Abuse of the drug or substance may lead to moderate or low-level physical dependence or high-level psychological dependence.

Schedule IV
- The drug or substance has a low potential for abuse relative to the drugs or substances in Schedule III.
- The drug or substance has a currently accepted medical use in the United States.
- Abuse of the drug or other substance may lead to limited physical dependence or psychological dependence relative to the drugs or other substances in Schedule III.

Schedule V
- The drug or substance has a low potential for abuse relative to the drugs or other substances in Schedule IV.
- The drug or substance has a currently accepted medical use in treatment in the United States.
- Abuse of the drug or substance may lead to limited physical dependence or psychological dependence relative to the drugs or other substances in Schedule IV.

Figure 6.1 Poster from the Reagan/Bush era "War on Drugs." *(National Library of Medicine)*

use. On the initial list, marijuana was classified along with heroin and LSD as a Schedule I drug, which identified the drug as having a high potential for abuse and no accepted medical use. Marijuana is still classified as a Schedule I drug and is still illegal under federal law. The Controlled Substance Act is considered one of the early laws in President Richard Nixon's "War on Drugs" because it gave a federal law enforcement agency—the Drug Enforcement Administration (DEA), formerly the Bureau of Narcotics and Dangerous Drugs—specific powers for fighting drug abuse in society.[2]

Since 1970, substances on the controlled substances list are determined by two federal agencies: the DEA and FDA.[3] A comprehensive listing of all controlled substances in the United States is included in Title 21 of the Code of Federal Regulation, a reference of all the rules and regulations of the federal government that is updated annually. According to the most current revision of the Code of Federal Regulations (April 2009), two synthetic cannabinoid drugs developed specifically for medical conditions—dronabinol and nabilone—are on the list of controlled substances. Dronabinol is classified as a Schedule III drug and nabilone is classified as Schedule II. Dronabinol was down classed from Schedule I to II in 1986, and again from Schedule II to III in 1999. Nabilone was added to the list as Schedule II in 1987. All the plant-derived tetrahydrocannabinoids (i.e., those contained in the cannabis plant) are included in Schedule I.[4]

U.S. drug policy shifted during the Ford and Carter presidential administrations (1974 to 1980), when policy makers weighed and engaged the public in discussions about the potential benefits of marijuana decriminalization. However, the Reagan and Bush administrations reversed the tide and intensified the "War on Drugs" (1981 to 1993), resulting in the passage of stricter laws and mandatory sentences for possession of marijuana.

FEDERAL LAWS

Marijuana use is illegal under federal law for any purpose, including its use as medicine. This is reflected in the U.S. Department of Justice's classification of marijuana as a Schedule I controlled substance. Possession, cultivation, and trafficking of marijuana are illegal and the penalties for each individual violation vary. Both federal and state laws divide offenses into two categories: (1) possession and (2) the more serious trafficking, selling, growing, and distributing.

Under federal law, possession of any amount of marijuana (even a single marijuana cigarette) is punishable by up to one year in prison (not jail) and a fine of $1,000 for a first offense; if the amount is less than an ounce, federal prosecutors have discretion to charge under the "personal use" statute. In this

THE WHITE HOUSE OFFICE OF NATIONAL DRUG CONTROL POLICY

Created by the Anti-Drug Abuse Act of 1988, under the Reagan administration, the Office of National Drug Control Policy (ONDCP) is a component of the Executive Office of the President. The purpose of ONDCP is to establish policies, priorities, and objectives for the drug control program in the United States. Specific goals of the program are to reduce the use, manufacturing, and trafficking of illicit drugs, and reduce drug-related crime, violence, and health consequences. ONDCP seeks to achieve these goals through the National Drug Control Strategy, which directs U.S. antidrug efforts and establishes a program, budget, and guidelines for cooperation among federal, state, and local entities.

By law, the director of ONDCP evaluates, coordinates, and oversees both the international and domestic antidrug efforts of executive branch agencies and ensures that such efforts sustain and complement state and local antidrug activities. The director advises the president regarding changes in the organization, management, budgeting, and personnel of federal agencies that could affect the nation's antidrug efforts, and regarding federal agency compliance with their obligations under the strategy.

case, possession is not treated as a crime but a civil offense, much like a traffic ticket (although the fine can be up to $10,000).[5] The second offense carries a 15-day mandatory sentence that can be extended for as long as two years in prison. Any possession after that gets a 90-day to three-year prison term and a $5,000 fine. Selling marijuana (trafficking) is considered a more serious crime with heavier penalties. (See Table 6.1.)

Under federal law, the medical use of marijuana is illegal. The DEA, in fulfilling its mission to enforce the Controlled Substances Act, has arrested hundreds of medical marijuana users and their caregivers for breaking the federal law.[6] However, in October 2009, a sudden shift in federal policy regarding prosecution of users and suppliers of medical marijuana occurred when the

Table 6.1 Federal Trafficking Penalties—Marijuana

QUANTITY	1st OFFENSE	2nd OFFENSE
1,000 kg or more mixture; or 1,000 or more plants	• Not less than 10 years, not more than life • If death or serious injury, not less than 20 years, not more than life • Fine not more than $4 million if an individual, $10 million if other than an individual	• Not less than 20 years, not more than life • If death or serious injury, mandatory life • Fine not more than $8 million if an individual, $20 million if other than an individual
100 kg to 999 kg mixture; or 100 to 999 plants	• Not less than 5 years, not more than 40 years • If death or serous injury, not less than 20 years, not more than life • Fine not more than $2 million if an individual, $5 million if other than an individual	• Not less than 10 years, not more than life • If death or serious injury, mandatory life • Fine not more than $4 million if an individual, $10 million if other than an individual
More than 10 kg hashish; 50 to 99 kg mixture more than 1 kg of hashish oil; 50 to 99 plants	• Not more than 20 years • If death or serous injury, not less than 20 years, not more than life • Fine $1 million if an individual, $5 million if other than an individual	• Not more than 30 years • If death or serious injury, mandatory life • Fine $2 million if an individual, $10 million if other than individual
Less than 50 kg mixture; 1 to 49 plants	• Not more than 5 years • Fine not more than $250,000, $1 million other than individual	• Not more than 10 years • Fine $500,000 if an individual, $2 million if other than individual

Source: U.S. Drug Enforcement Administration, http://www.justice.gov/dea/agency/penalties.htm

Justice Department announced that it would not prosecute users or suppliers of medical marijuana in states where it is legal as long as they are in accordance with the state marijuana laws.

STATE LAWS

State laws regarding marijuana vary. Since 1973, 10 states have decriminalized possession and use of small amounts of marijuana: Alaska, Colorado, California, Mississippi, North Carolina, New York, Nebraska, Nevada, Ohio, and Oregon. Decriminalization only lessens the penalty to a fine (in many states). Also, since 1996, medical marijuana laws have been passed in 14 states and the District of Columbia. (See Table 6.2) With the exception of Maryland, all criminal penalties are removed for patients who use marijuana. However, Maryland's law does not legalize possession of medical marijuana, but makes it an offense with no jail and a maximum penalty of a $100 fine. In all of these states except New Jersey, patients can legally grow their own marijuana, or get it from a caregiver or a licensed provider.

CRIMES AND PUNISHMENTS

According to the Federal Bureau of Investigation's Uniform Crime Reporting Program, an estimated 1,702,537 state and local arrests for drug-abuse violations were made in the United States during 2008. Of these drug-abuse violation arrests, 5.5% were for the sale and/or manufacture of marijuana and 44.3% were for marijuana possession.[7] In contrast, there were 6,337 federal arrests for marijuana-related charges during 2008. Of these, about 97.8% involved trafficking and 1.6% involved simple possession.[8] A recent study found that the explosion in marijuana-related arrests in the 1990's did not decrease the use (nearly all of the growth in arrests during that period was for possession), availability, or cost of marijuana.[9] Additionally, the cost of this effort, which was significant, might be considered wasted because it did not impact the recreational use of marijuana. The study authors concluded that the current approach wastes valuable law enforcement and court system resources.

There is a current movement to develop more innovative programs for first-time offenders such as alternative sentencing. One such strategy is a called "adjournment in contemplation for dismissal," a form of pretrial probation

| Table 6.2 States Legalizing Medical Marijuana ||
States	Year Law Passed
Alaska	1998
California	1996
Colorado	2000
District of Columbia	2010
Hawaii	2000
Maine	1999
Michigan	2008
Montana	2004
Nevada	2000
New Jersey	2010
New Mexico	2007
Oregon	1998
Rhode Island	2006
Vermont	2004
Washington	1998

Source: ProCon.org, http://medicalmarijuana.procon.org/view.resource.php?resourceID=000881.

which keeps first-time offenders out of jail. Here's how it works: In exchange for a promise not to violate the terms of their probation, the offender does no jail time. After the prescribed time period, assuming no violation, all charges are dismissed and there is no criminal record. About 23 states have such programs with some variations. Another strategy is drug courts for adults and juveniles. Drug courts offer treatment and community service as alternatives to jail.[10]

LEGALIZATION EFFORTS

The debate over the legal status of marijuana continues. Advocates for legalization argue that marijuana is a safe drug and that criminal penalties for personal use and possession should be reformed. Opponents of legalization argue that marijuana is not a safe drug and that either legalizing or decriminalizing personal use would trigger a substantial increase in use, with foreseeable increases in social, economic, and health costs. Most recently, the debate has focused on the medical use of marijuana.

There is a groundswell of grassroots support for the reform of marijuana laws, including The National Organization for the Reform of Marijuana Laws (NORML), the Marijuana Policy Project, and Americans for Safe Access. Additionally, prestigious medical organizations such as the American Medical Association and the American College of Physicians have endorsed the use of medical marijuana. A number of states have recognized marijuana's medical value and have either passed or adopted laws legalizing the use of medical marijuana. Since federal policy has a significant impact on the laws, the recent shift in federal government policy regarding medical marijuana use may herald a more favorable environment for reform of marijuana laws.

7
Marijuana Medicinal or Therapeutic Uses

Rachel Mittal's mother, diagnosed with "primary progressive multiple sclerosis" (MS) at age 32, had recently been coping really well with her MS symptoms. The bouts of spasticity (involuntary rapid muscle contractions), tremors, and uncoordinated movement, which affected her mother's walking to the degree that sometimes she had to rely on a wheelchair to get around, were unpredictable in their frequency. Rachel, her brother, and her dad, and her mom, of course, felt like they had become experts on MS after her mother had participated in two clinical trials where new MS drugs were being tested in patients. Although there is no cure, some medications and treatment regimens, including investigative treatments combined with intense physical therapy, prolong the time between episodes and the recovery from episodes is better quantitatively and qualitatively.

Searching for a snack one day, Rachel hesitated when she came across a clear plastic sandwich bag of brownies labeled "MOM ONLY." Rachel yelled out to her mother to ask what this was about, and could she please have some. Her mother zoomed into the kitchen in her wheelchair, taking Rachel by surprise, screaming, "No, they're mine, they're only for me." Rachel had never seen her mother so agitated; her reaction was so out of proportion to the situation. Rachel automatically asked, "What's wrong? I didn't eat any. I just asked. And since when do you label food as 'MOM ONLY'?" On realizing that she needed to come clean with her teenage daughter, Rachel's mom explained that her last relapse happened while she was on an experimental MS medication.

It wasn't good, and the muscle spasms were becoming more frequent and debilitating, so the doctor suggested trying marijuana since all other therapeutic options have been pretty much exhausted. Rachel cut her mom off and said, "Mom, I know a lot about medical marijuana. You didn't need to hide it from me. Does Dad know? Does Claymont? I hope you're not ashamed about it. Can you tell if the muscle relaxing effects of the marijuana brownies are working? Wait, that's what's been allowing you to walk around without a wheelchair in the mornings?"Rachel's mom answered, "It must be. I eat the brownies in the evenings so that I don't have any of the foggy brain effects of marijuana. I don't want that."

Marijuana as a painkiller, antiemetic (for nausea and vomiting), muscle relaxant, and appetite stimulant cannot be dismissed as a fringe medical practice. Treating acute or chronic pain, nausea and vomiting, muscle **spasticity**, and loss of appetite and unintended weight loss with marijuana or its active ingredient, tetrahydrocannabinol or THC, does have scientific merit. The history of marijuana use for therapeutic purposes spans millennia, but only in the 1980s and 1990s did advances in molecular biology and pharmacology reveal *how* marijuana exerts its effects, beginning with the discovery of cell surface receptors that bind the THC molecule (the cannabinoid receptors CB1 and CB2 in the central nervous system) and the molecular and cellular events following the binding interaction. Recall from Chapter 3 that the phytocannabinoids including THC extracted from the *Cannabis sativa* plant, the naturally occurring, or endogenous, cannabinoids in the body (endocannabinoids), and synthetic cannabinoids interact with CB1 and CB2 receptors on the surface of select cells, including neurons, endothelial cells, and immune system cells, ultimately resulting in highly specific and quantifiable physiologic effects (e.g., rapid heart rate, increased blood pressure, slurred speech). Laboratory researchers continue to conduct experiments to more precisely define the action of THC at the biochemical and molecular level: the cast of enzymes involved in the metabolism of THC and other cannabinoids, the differential number and proportion of functional CB1 and CB2 receptors on various cell types in different physiologic and pathologic states, the signaling molecules, and the diffusion and transport patterns across cell membranes in different tissues.

Modern scientific investigation into the potential therapeutic uses of marijuana essentially began after cannabinoids were isolated and characterized in the 1960s. Interest in marijuana as medicine intensified among academic and

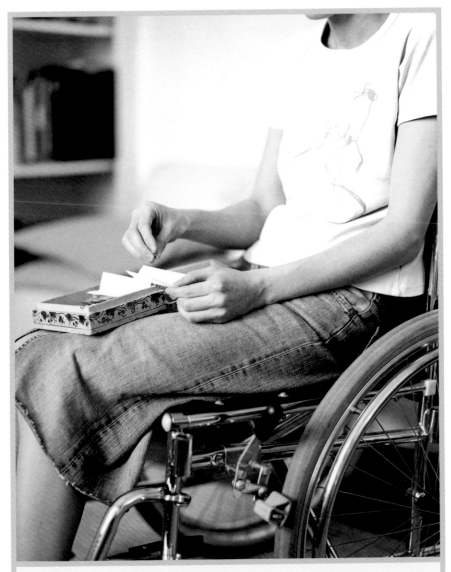

Figure 7.1 A woman with advanced multiple sclerosis prepares a cannabis cigarette. (© *Lee Powers/ Photo Researchers, Inc.*)

pharmaceutical scientists in the 1990s, coinciding with the discovery of the endocannabinoid system and the elucidation of the mechanisms of action of THC. With this newfound knowledge, researchers set to the task of identifying and synthesizing compounds that act on the CB1 receptor. Every major pharmaceutical company and some not-so-big ones are engaged in exploiting the endocannabinoid system to develop medicines. Laboratory experiments, preclinical trials in animal models, and clinical trials are being conducted to evaluate smoked marijuana and THC or other cannabinoid-containing drugs or products for their efficacy and safety in patients with various conditions and diseases.

MEDICAL MARIJUANA'S HISTORY

Marijuana has been used to treat a variety of medical conditions since at least 2700 B.C.. The earliest known written description of the therapeutic properties of the *Cannabis sativa* plant appeared in the world's oldest compendium of medicines and drug preparations, the Chinese pharmacopoeia known as the *Pen Ts'ao Ching*. The ancient Chinese appeared to have used cannabis for pain and as an anaesthetic for surgery, for constipation, **beriberi** (thiamine or vitamin B1 deficiency), menstrual cramps and labor pains, malaria, **gout**, and absentmindedness. In Africa and the Middle East, marijuana was used to treat fever, blood poisoning, anthrax, snake bites, malaria, fluid retention, gout, gastrointestinal discomfort, toothaches, earaches, asthma, **dysentery**, epileptic seizures, and according to an Arabian medical text in the year A.D. 1000, to "clean the brain." Perhaps most consistently throughout history, marijuana's calming or sedative effects have been exploited to treat anxiety-related psychiatric disorders.[1]

In 1652, the noted British physician and herbalist Nicholas Culpeper wrote about the medicinal properties of extracts from the cannabis plant, indicating that an extract can allay headaches and ease the pains of gout and arthritis. In the early 1800s, scientists in Napoléon Bonaparte's army returned home from a military campaign in Egypt with the cannabis plant and studied its properties based on their observations and experiences in Egypt. The scientists published their findings in a French medical journal in 1809, sparking interest in marijuana in the medical field (alcohol-based tinctures and poultices containing cannabis for use as a home remedy) and in society (as a recreational intoxicant). Sir William O'Shaughnessy, an Irish physician, who worked in Calcutta with the British army, is credited with publishing the first scientific study of cannabis in 1839.[2] O'Shaughnessy apparently read everything available on the cannabis plant, described the various forms of preparations in use in India, evaluated the effects of increasing doses in animals, and ultimately tested cannabis preparation in patients with rheumatism, convulsions, and muscular spasms from tetanus and rabies. In his article, "On the preparations of the Indian hemp, or gunjah," O'Shaughnessy writes:

> The narcotic effects of Hemp are popularly known in the south of Africa, South America, Turkey, Egypt, Middle East Asia, India, and the adjacent territories of the Malays, Burmese, and Siamese. In all these countries, Hemp is used in various forms, by the dissipated and depraved, as the ready agent of a pleasing intoxication. In the popular medicine of these nations, we find it extensively employed for a multitude of affections. But in Western Europe, its use either as a stimulant or as a remedy is equally unknown.

In 1845, Jacques-Joseph Moreau, a French psychiatrist, provided one of the most complete descriptions of the psychoactive properties and therapeutic

Figure 7.2 A bottle of cannabis tincture that was once available by prescription. (© David Hoffman Photo Library/ Alamy)

MARIJUANA AND NINETEENTH-CENTURY PSYCHIATRY

Jacques-Joseph Moreau (1804–1884), a French psychiatrist, was one pioneer in the field of psychiatry who focused on the functional basis of insanity rather than its structural (anatomic) basis. Moreau worked with institutionalized psychiatric patients at the Charenton Asylum, near Paris, and traveled with these patients to exotic and distant countries, as was the practice of the times. He observed the apparently common use of hashish (cannabis resin) among Arabs and the substance's effects. Moreau's scientific background allowed him to see a connection between the behaviors of cannabis users and those of some insane or "mad" patients. Back in Paris, Moreau conducted experiments using different cannabis preparations, first on himself and later on his students. In 1845 he published the book, *Du Hachisch et de l'Alienation Mentale: Etudes Psychologiques* (Hashish and Mental Illness), providing one of the most complete descriptions of the acute effects of cannabis. Moreau observed that hashish induced some of the same hallucinations and disordered thoughts that he saw in his psychiatric patients, which led him to hypothesize about the under-

uses of cannabis in a book on mental illness.[3] The interest in marijuana's medicinal properties in the Western world in the 1800s was undoubtedly due to the scarcity of therapeutic options for such common infectious diseases as rabies, cholera, and tetanus. In 1860, the first clinical conference focused on cannabis took place in the United States, and by 1880, British, German, and U.S. pharmaceutical companies—E. Merck (now Merck & Co.), Sharpe & Dohm Co. (now Merck & Co.), Squibb (now Bristol-Myers Squibb), Burroughs-Wellcome & Co. (now Glaxo Wellcome), Parke-Davis (now Pfizer Inc.), and Eli Lilly—were marketing cannabis powdered extracts (e.g., *Cannabinum tannicum Merck*) or tinctures.[4]

By the early 1900s, three broad therapeutic categories for marijuana preparations were recognized in Western medicine: as a sedative or hypnotic agent, an analgesic, and "other," which included appetite stimulant.[5] Tincture of cannabis BPC (British Pharmaceutical Codex) was listed in the British pinnings of insanity: "I saw in hashish, more specifically in its effects on mental abilities, a powerful and unique method to investigate the genesis of mental illness." Moreau's experiments led him to conclude that insanity resulted from a disturbance in brain function that caused an unbalanced state. Moreau's systematic experiments with hashish and his writings contributed to the continued study and investigation of the etiology and treatment of mental illness. Cannabis' diverse effects on the central nervous system—altered memory and sensory and time perception, altered coordination, fatigue and sleepiness, euphoria or dysphoria, visual and/or auditory hallucinations, onset of anxiety or reduced anxiety, slurred speech, enhanced creativity—and their resemblance to behaviors associated with specific psychiatric diagnoses are well appreciated today by life scientists and social sciences in numerous specialties, not only psychiatrists.

E.L. Abel, "Jacques Joseph Moreau (1804–1884): Images in Psychiatry," *American Journal of Psychiatry* 162, 3 (March 2005), http://ajp.psychiatryonline.org (accessed January 17, 2009); J-J Moreau, *Hashish and Mental Illness.* (Paris: Librarie de Fortin Masson, 1845); E. Russo. "Cognoscenti of Cannabis I: Jacques-Joseph Moreau (1804–1884)," *Journal of Cannabis Therapeutics* 1, 1 (2001): 85–88; A.W. Zuardi, "History of *Cannabis* as a Medicine: A Review," *Revista Brasileira de Psiquiatr* 28, 2 (2006): 153–157.

Pharmacopoeia from 1864 to 1942, but remained available by prescription in the United Kingdom until 1971.[6] In the United States, marijuana was listed in the *U.S. Pharmacopoeia* from 1851 until 1942 and was prescribed for various conditions, including labor pains, nausea, and rheumatism. Although cannabis preparations provided symptomatic relief in a variety of medical conditions, they were never considered or billed as a cure for any disease or condition. Following government campaigns against the use of cannabis begun in the 1930s, medicinal extracts and tinctures were removed from pharmacopoeias in industrialized countries.

MEDICAL MARIJUANA TODAY

Medical marijuana includes smoking the dried mature flowers and leaves of cultivated *Cannabis sativa* plants (no different from that smoked by

Table 7.1: Early Twentieth-Century Medical Uses of Marijuana	
Cannabis preparations: Therapeutic categories	Uses
Sedative or hypnotic agent	insomnia, senile insomnia, melancholia, mania, delirium tremens, chorea, tetanus, rabies, hay fever, bronchitis, pulmonary tuberculosis, cough, paralysis agitans (Parkinson's disease), exophthalmic goiter, spasm of the bladder, gonorrhea
Analgesic	headaches, migraine, eyestrain, menopause, brain tumors, tic douloureux, neuralgia, gastric ulcer, gastralgia (indigestion), tabes (wasting), multiple neuritis, pain not due to lesions, uterine disturbances, dysmenorrhea, chronic inflammation, menorrhagia, impending abortion, postpartum hemorrhage, acute rheumatism, eczema, senile pruritus (itching), tingling, formication (a crawling sensation) and numbness of gout, dental pain
Other	To improve appetite and digestion, for the "pronounced anorexia following exhausting diseases," gastric neuroses, dyspepsia, diarrhea, dysentery, cholera, nephritis (kidney inflammation), hematuria (blood in the urine), diabetes mellitus, cardiac palpitation, vertigo, female sexual atony, male impotence

Source: Charles E. de M. Sajous, M.D., Analytic Cyclopedia of Practical Medicine (F.A. Davis Company, 1924).

recreational marijuana users). In addition, several pharmaceutical-grade products, sometimes referred to as cannabis-based medicine, are recognized for their clinical benefit by the medical community and have been approved for use for specific conditions by drug regulatory agencies in the United States and other countries. These include:

- dronabinol (Marinol): a synthetic form of oral THC available as capsules
- delta-9-tetrahydrocannabinol with cannabidiol (Sativex): an extract preparation from the *Cannabis sativa* plant available as buccal

(inside the cheeks), oromucosal (oral cavity), or sublingual (under the tongue) spray

- nabilone (Cesamet): a synthetic cannabinoid (derivative of THC) available in capsule form

Table 7.2. Diseases and Conditions for which Marijuana or THC-containing Products are Currently Used or Being Investigated as Treatments	
Diseases	
• Cancer	• Arthritis / rheumatoid arthritis
• HIV/AIDS	• Asthma
• Multiple sclerosis	• Epilepsy
• Glaucoma	• Fibromyalgia
• Stroke	• Parkinson's disease
• Alzheimer's disease	• Tourette syndrome
• Retinal diseases (including diabetic retinopathy)	• Amyotrophic lateral sclerosis (ALS), also known as Lou Gehrig's disease
• Crohn's disease (colitis)	• Granulomatous amebic encephalitis
• Chronic liver diseases	• Inflammatory diseases
Specific Conditions	
• Acute postoperative pain	• Neuropathic pain
• Cancer pain	• Menstrual discomfort
• Migraine headache	• Labor pains
• Joint pain	• Nausea and vomiting
• Chronic pain	• Muscle spasms
• Anorexia associated with unintended weight loss in HIV/AIDS patients	• Seizures
• Cachexia (malnutrition and wasting)	• Obesity
• Acute liver injury	• Osteoporosis
• Autism	• Drug dependence (e.g., opioid dependence)

At this time, in the United States, dronabinol and nabilone are the only FDA-approved cannabinoid-based drugs. Both drugs are approved to reduce cancer chemotherapy–induced nausea and vomiting; dronabinol is also

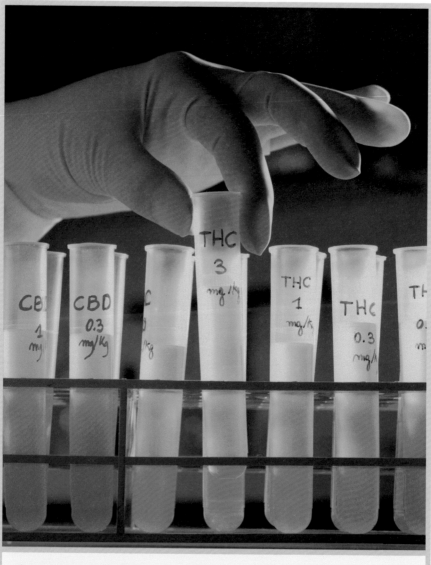

Figure 7.3 Cannabis researcher with various compounds found in cannabis, including THC. (©Mauro Fermariello/ Photo Researchers, Inc.)

approved to stimulate appetite in HIV/AIDS patients (for HIV-associated "wasting" or anorexia). In Canada only, delta-9-tetahydrocannabinol with cannabidiol is "conditionally approved" for **neuropathic pain** in multiple sclerosis and for cancer pain. Although THC-based medicines are being evaluated for a number of conditions and diseases, the approved indications for use by drug regulatory agencies are quite limited. The list of conditions for which medical marijuana may be beneficial continues to grow as more is

TARGETING THE CB2 CANNABINOID RECEPTOR

Not all products that act on the CB1 and/or CB2 receptors are cannabinoids. For example, the investigative agent, Sch35966, originally in development as a treatment for analgesia, is not a cannabinoid; it belongs to the benzoquinolizinone class of drugs, which are primarily used to treat anxiety disorders. Animal studies conducted by the U.S. drug manufacturer Schering-Plough (now Merck & Co.) in 2006–2007 showed that Sch35966 acts by selectively binding to the CB2 receptor, which is found primarily on immune system cells. Another CB2-specific receptor agonist that is not a cannabinoid is the investigative agent Sch414319, which belongs to a new class of compounds described as triaryl bis-sulfones. Like Sch35966, this newer investigative compound has little or no binding affinity for CB1 receptors and is therefore an attractive therapeutic agent because it targets immunomodulation (e.g., anti-inflammatory processes) without affecting behavioral and cognitive functions mediated by CB1 receptors. This means fewer psychoactive side effects with CB2 receptor-specific agonists. Studies examining the mechanism of action of Sch414319 in different animal models suggest that this drug (or related compounds in the same class with potent and selective binding to CB2) will have a role in treating arthritis and autoimmune diseases.

W. Gonsiorek et al., "Sch35966 is a Potent, Selective Agonist at the Peripheral Cannabinoid Receptor (CB2) in Rodents and Primates," British Journal of Pharmacology 151 (2007): 1262–1271; C.A. Lunn et al., "Biology and Therapeutic Potential of Cannabinoid CB2 Receptor Inverse Agonists," British Journal of Pharmacology 153, 2 (January 2008): 226–239.

learned about the endocannabinoid system and the interrelationships with specific organs and tissues.

The range of medical marijuana products either approved for use by drug regulatory agencies (and therefore permissible for use by prescription under state and federal law) or in the experimental preclinical and clinical investigation stages includes preparations of natural purified compounds from the *Cannabis sativa* plant, synthetic THC, other synthetic cannabinoids and cannabinoid analogs (chemical look-alikes), and compounds that act on CB1 and/or CB2 receptors. The mechanism of action of the majority of cannabis-based medicines is by binding with the CB1 and/or CB2 receptors as agonists or antagonists, eliciting or inhibiting specific physiologic effects, respectively.

In addition to the evaluation of the efficacy and toxicity or safety of cannabis-based medicines, pharmaceutical scientists are also testing various routes of administration for these products to optimize the delivery of THC to target tissues. Drug delivery systems, which include traditional pill formulations, affect the timing of drug action and distribution to different tissues, drug concentration in different compartments, and the half-life and elimination of the parent compound. Thus, there may be pharmacokinetic advantages associated with specific routes of administration for THC. Drug delivery systems for THC-based medicines that have been investigated include pills, smoking, vaporization (smokeless cigarettes), aerosolized particulate devices (nasal and oromucosal sprays and metered-dose inhalers), intravenous administration, transdermal patches, and rectal suppositories. The intravenous route of administration of THC has only been studied for research purposes, but is considered a practical approach for therapeutics. One of the key advantages of oromucosal, transcutaneous, and rectal routes of administration is that more of the parent compound can be delivered directly to the intended target tissues without being degraded. Pharmacologists have long wrestled with the challenge of smoking as an inhalation drug delivery system because of the technical difficulty in standardizing dose; however, as discussed in Chapter 3, the onset of drug action with smoking marijuana is rapid. The oral route of administration has a slow onset of action.

SMOKED MARIJUANA FOR THERAPEUTIC USES

According to the American Medical Association, less than 20, relatively small, randomized controlled clinical trials of short duration involving approximately 300 patients have been conducted over the last 35 years on smoked marijuana. Results from these trials indicate that smoked marijuana does reduce neuropathic pain, improve appetite and caloric intake (especially in patients with reduced muscle mass), and may relieve spasticity and pain in patients with multiple sclerosis.

Marijuana and marijuana cigarettes are not approved by the FDA for use as a treatment for any disease or condition. However, beginning in 1978, the FDA allowed the medical use of marijuana under its Compassionate Use Investigational New Drug program. Patients enrolled in this program could receive marijuana from the National Institute on Drug Abuse, one of the institutes of the U.S. National Institutes of Health. A laboratory at the University of Mississippi was contracted to grow, harvest, process, and ship marijuana to licensed facilities across the United States for research purposes and to individual patients enrolled in the compassionate use program. Despite the closing of the program in 1992, those individuals still living who were in the program in 1992 continue to receive marijuana from the government.

Several states have medical marijuana laws that allow the possession and use of marijuana for medical purposes, although the particulars of each state's laws vary.

In Canada, marijuana is not approved as a treatment for any conditions by the regulatory agency under Health Canada. However, in 2001, the "Marihuana medical access regulations" were instated to allow seriously ill patients residing in Canada to obtain authorization to possess or produce marijuana for medical reasons.

SMOKELESS MARIJUANA

One primary disadvantage of smoking marijuana for therapeutic benefit is smoking itself. As pharmacologists put it, "inhalation of a combustion product is an undesirable delivery system." The harmful effects of smoking and the difficulty in administering a uniform dose with smoking, combined with the advantageous rapid onset of drug action associated with inhalation, have led to the pursuit of alternative inhalation routes. A vaporization device called Volcano (manufactured by the German company, Storz & Bickel) has been shown to deliver levels of THC comparable to those delivered from smoking marijuana cigarettes. In a study of 18 healthy adult volunteers, peak plasma

THE CURIOUS CASE OF BOB RANDALL

In 1976, Bob Randall, a young man with severe glaucoma, was prosecuted for marijuana possession in the District of Columbia. At his trial, Randall's doctors testified that the patient's disease was not responding to conventional therapies and that he risked going blind without marijuana to relieve the pressure in his eyes. He was found not guilty by reason of medical necessity. Randall brought a civil suit against the government for legal access to marijuana, and in 1978, Randall and the government reached a settlement: The government agreed to supply Randall with marijuana for the rest of his life!

The government made the deal because the National Institute on Drug Abuse was growing small quantities of marijuana for research purposes under contract with the University of Mississippi's pharmacy school, and could lawfully become Randall's supplier if he were part of a clinical study. So he was enrolled in a clinical trial with just one patient—himself—and a research "protocol" was developed.

The 1978 settlement in the case became the legal basis for the FDA's Compassionate Use Investigational New Drug program. By 1991, the compassionate-use program had grown to include 13 patients. Although the government shut down the program in 1992, those 13 patients were grandfathered in and those still alive continue to receive marijuana from the U.S. government, legally.

Roger Parloff, "How Marijuana Became Legal," *Fortune Magazine*, September 11, 2009, http://money.cnn.com/2009/09/11/magazines/fortune/medical_marijuana_legalizing.fortune/ (accessed September 30, 2010).

THC concentrations and THC exposure over time with vaporized THC were found to be similar to values achieved with smoked THC. However, study participants randomly chosen for the vaporized THC group had lower expired carbon monoxide levels compared with the smoked THC group. No adverse events were reported. Although this pilot study appears to have documented that vaporization of cannabis is a safe and effective delivery system of THC, it does not appear that additional U.S. trials are slated to further evaluate the clinical effectiveness of this smokeless delivery system.[7]

PLANT-DERIVED THC AND THC-CONTAINING PRODUCT: DELTA-9-TETAHYDROCANNABINOL WITH CANNABIDIOL

Seventy percent of delta-9-tetahydrocannabinol with cannabidiol (trade name Sativex) is composed of equal proportions of THC and cannabidiol, two genetically characterized phytocannabinoids from the *Cannabis sativa* plant, and the remaining 30% of this extract consists of other cannabinoids and other compounds from the *Cannabis sativa* plant. The manufacturer of this product, based in the United Kingdom, has been growing pesticide-free *Cannabis sativa L.* plants in secure, climate-controlled greenhouses under a licensing agreement with the British government since 1998. GW Pharmaceuticals employs experts in horticulture and genetics to breed cloned plants to ensure consistency in the composition and ratio of individual cannabinoids in each plant.[8]

Delta-9-tetahydrocannabinol with cannabidiol is administered directly under the tongue (oromucosally) or inside of the cheeks (buccally). The beauty of the oromucosal spray formulation is that it delivers unaltered parent compounds to the intended target tissues (i.e., CB1 and CB2 receptors in the central nervous system and immune system), and drug absorption into the bloodstream through the oral mucosa is immediate. (For oral pill formulations, drug absorption occurs in the gastrointestinal tract after the pill is swallowed; the parent compound may be partially degraded in the digestive system.)

Sativex is not an approved medicine in the United States; however, it received conditional authorization for use as buccal spray in Canada in 2005 for the treatment of neuropathic pain associated with multiple sclerosis, and is authorized in three European countries for a number of indications. According to the notification letter of conditional authorization in 2005, Sativex may be useful as adjunctive analgesic treatment in adult multiple sclerosis patients with neuropathic pain. Conditional marketing approval by Health Canada was based on a four-week placebo-controlled clinical trial in which significant reduction in pain scores and improved sleep were found in patients with multiple sclerosis who had neuropathic pain of at least three months' duration. Delta-9-tetahydrocannabinol with cannabidiol is not approved for use in adolescents or children under 18 years of age because safety and efficacy have not been determined in these groups.

THC is highly bound to plasma proteins and therefore delta-9-tetahydrocannabinol with cannabidiol may displace other drugs that are highly plasma-protein bound, potentially resulting in unintended and harmful drug-drug interactions. In addition, patients taking drugs that are metabolized by CYP450 2D6 and/or CYP450 3A4, such as the prescription pain medication fentanyl and the related opioids sufentanil and alfentanil, may experience increased effects of these drugs. THC inhibits the activity of CYP450 metabolism, and therefore drugs that are normally metabolized by these enzymes are more slowly or less completely metabolized and consequently may have greater exposure in the systemic circulation for a longer period of time. There is also a possible interaction with the antidepressant amitriptyline, because it is metabolized by CYP2C19, CYP1A2, CYP2C9, CYP3A4, and CYP2D6: taking amitriptyline with delta-9-tetrahydrocannabinol with cannabidiol could lead to raised plasma levels of amitriptyline. Although the pharmacokinetics of the delta-9-tetrahydrocannabinol with cannabidiol product suggest that these drug-drug interactions could occur, there have been no clinical reports documenting such interactions in patients. The main side effects of delta-9-tetahydrocannabinol with cannabidiol are mouth irritations (dry mouth or stinging) and intoxication, including dizziness when first taken, disorientation, impaired memory, disturbance in attention, drowsiness, dissociation, and euphoric mood.

SYNTHETIC THC AND THC-BASED PRODUCTS: DRONABINOL AND NABIOLONE

Dronabinol (trade name Marinol) is the international nonproprietary name for synthetic THC; it was the first synthetic THC product available commercially for therapeutic use. Clinical testing of dronabinol capsules began in the 1970s, and the drug was formally approved by the FDA in 1985 to reduce cancer chemotherapy–induced nausea and vomiting and to stimulate appetite in HIV-associated anorexia or wasting. Dronabinol is approved for use in pediatric patients, but only for the treatment of chemotherapy-induced emesis and not for AIDS-related anorexia because the drug has not been evaluated in clinical trials with HIV/AIDS pediatric patients. Dronabinol is also available by prescription in Canada, the United Kingdom, Germany, and Austria. In the United States, dronabinol is a controlled substance and is classified as a

Schedule III drug under the Controlled Substances Act, which indicates that there is some potential for abuse.

Pharmacologic studies have shown that after ingesting one capsule (a single oral dose), dronabinol is almost completely absorbed by the gastro-intestinal tract, although only 10% to 20% of the dose reaches the systemic circulation because of extensive metabolism by the liver. These studies were conducted in healthy volunteers in the fasted condition (i.e., before a break-fast meal), and it is not known if the absorption of dronabinol is affected if taken with a meal or shortly before or after a meal.

What about taking dronabinol with other medications? There are poten-tial drug-drug interactions when certain drugs—medicines as well as drugs of abuse—are taken in the same time frame as dronabinol. The combina-tion of dronabinol and stimulants, such as amphetamines and cocaine, for example, can lead to additive adverse cardiac effects (increased blood pres-sure and rapid heartbeat); note that drugs used to treat attention-deficit/hyperactivity disorder (ADHD) include amphetamines. Any drugs that act to depress central nervous system functioning, including smoked cannabis, alcohol, and sedatives (including codeine and other opioids), should not be taken with dronabinol because of additive depressant effects. Such drug combinations can lead to extreme drug-drug interactions due to changes in the bioavailability of dronabinol and/or the bioavailability of the coadmin-istered drug. Dronabinol is said to be a highly plasma protein-bound drug, which means that once dronabinol is absorbed into the bloodstream, plasma proteins glom onto the drug, which in effect reduces the bioavailability of the drug (i.e., less "free drug" is available to act on its intended target tissue). As a highly protein-bound drug, dronabinol may displace other plasma protein-bound drugs, thereby increasing the bioavailability of other coad-ministered medications, resulting in a too-powerful dose. Of course, it works both ways: the bioavailability of dronabinol can be increased through protein displacement by coadministered drugs that are themselves protein-bound. Some common plasma protein-bound drugs include the anti-inflammatory pain reliever ibuprofen, anticancer drug Taxol (paclitaxel), the antiseizure drugs phenytoin and valproic acid, and numerous antiretroviral drugs for HIV/AIDS.

Like most aspects of medicine, prescribing dronabinol is part science and part art. There is significant variation among individuals in the response

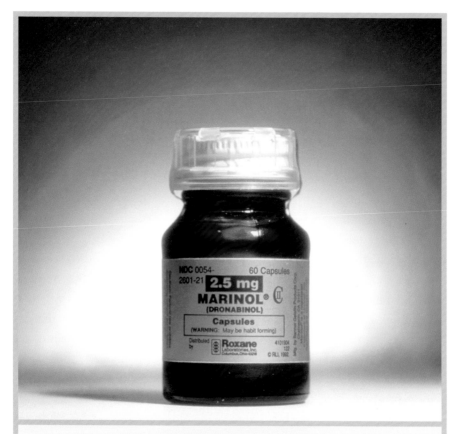

Figure 7.4 Dronabinol, trade name Marinol, a synthetic cannibinoid used medically as an appetite stimulant for AIDS sufferers. *(© Time & Life Pictures / Getty Images)*

and tolerability to dronabinol's effects. The complete prescribing information from the drug manufacturer warns that dronabinol should be used with caution in specific patient populations, including those with a history of seizures or tic disorders, those with cardiac disorders, those with mental illness, and those with a history of substance dependence or substance abuse. Dronabinol should also be used with caution in elderly patients because of potentially greater sensitivity to its psychoactive and hypotensive effects. Common dose-related side effects of dronabinol are those associated with marijuana's euphoric effect: "easy laughing, elation, and heightened awareness." Other adverse effects include abdominal pain, nausea, vomiting, dizziness, paranoid reaction, drowsiness, and abnormal thinking.

Clinical trials continue to evaluate the safety and efficacy of dronabinol in specific patient populations and for conditions not specifically or not yet approved by the FDA. One example is a randomized, placebo-controlled trial of dronabinol for the treatment of muscle cramps in amyotrophic lateral sclerosis (Lou Gehrig's disease). At this time, no single medication provides a lasting clinical benefit for painful muscle cramps, although according to anecdotal information, several are used to varying degrees of success.[9] Another clinical trial is exploring the potential role of dronabinol to help treat addiction to heroin and other opioids. In this two-year trial, begun in January 2010, dronabinol is being tested as an adjunct treatment with naltrexone, the FDA-approved medication for alcohol and opioid drug dependence. Dronabinol is administered during the initial detoxification period and during the first five weeks of naltrexone treatment to improve the tolerability of naltrexone and thereby facilitate the ability of patients to adhere to the treatment regimen. Upon acceptance, the trial participants—adult men and women with opioid dependence—are randomized into one of two treatment groups: naltrexone plus placebo or naltrexone plus dronabinol.[10]

The synthetic cannabinoid nabilone (trade name Cesamet) is chemically very similar to THC: the chemical formula of THC is $C_{21}H_{30}O_2$ and that of nabilone is $C_{24}H_{36}O_3$. Nabilone was approved by the FDA in 1985 to reduce chemotherapy-induced nausea and vomiting in patients unable to tolerate conventional antiemetic agents. Nabilone is also available in Canada, as well as the United Kingdom and several other European countries. Nabilone's primary effect is on the gastrointestinal tract, but it also has mood- and mind-altering central nervous system effects, producing relaxation, drowsiness, and euphoria at the recommended dosage. Nabilone is a controlled substance, specifically a Schedule II narcotic under the Controlled Substances Act (see Chapter 6). Schedule II substances have a high potential for abuse, and therefore health-care providers need to monitor patients receiving nabilone for signs of excessive use, abuse, and misuse. Because of the abuse potential, nabilone prescriptions are limited to the amount necessary for a single cycle of chemotherapy (typically 3 to 10 days). Nabilone is not approved for use in adolescents or children younger than 18 years of age because safety and efficacy have not been determined in these groups.

The absorption of nabilone is not affected by food, and therefore nabilone capsules can be taken before or after a meal or on an empty stomach. Nabilone should not be taken with alcohol, smoked marijuana, sedatives, or any drugs that depress central nervous system functioning (e.g., codeine or diazepam) because of additive depressant effects. Other drug-drug interactions cannot be ruled out because nabilone is highly bound to plasma proteins. Like dronabinol and plant-derived THC, which are also highly plasma-protein bound, nabilone could displace plasma proteins from other drugs that are themselves highly bound to plasma proteins; such displacement increases the unbound drug concentration of coadministered medications or recreational drugs and therefore possibly heightening their effects. The converse is also true, such that the free drug concentration of nabilone is increased by protein displacement by coadministered drugs that are highly plasma-protein bound. The most common side effects of nabilone are drowsiness, vertigo, dry mouth, low blood pressure, elevated heart rate, euphoria, impaired coordination, headache, and difficulty concentrating.

Ongoing clinical trials are evaluating nabilone for its safety and efficacy for specific pain conditions and symptoms related to those conditions. For

(*continues on page 105*)

Table 7.3. Investigative Cannabinoid Agents and/or CB Receptor Ligands[11]			
Agent	Classification	Receptor target and activity	Therapeutic target
SAB378	Synthetic cannabinoid	CB1 agonist	Neuropathic pain
Rimonabant (SR141716)	Synthetic cannabinoid	CB1 antagonist	Alcohol, marijuana, and other drug dependence
AM1241	Aminoalkylindole (non-cannabinoid)	CB2 agonist	Analgesia; neuropathic pain
ACEA (arachidonoyl 2'-chloroethylamide)	Endocannabinoid	CB1 agonist	Multiple sclerosis; myocardial infarction

U.S. FOOD AND DRUG ADMINISTRATION APPROVAL PROCESS FOR DRUGS

The Food and Drug Administration (FDA) is the federal agency responsible for ensuring the safety and effectiveness of drugs. New drugs that are discovered and tested by pharmaceutical companies, government or private biomedical research organizations, or universities or academic medical centers must undergo formal evaluation by the FDA. The review process lasts about seven years on average. However, many drug candidates that undergo preclinical (in vitro and animal) testing never make it to human testing, and the majority of drugs that are clinically evaluated in humans do not make it to pharmacy shelves. It takes approximately 10 to 15 years, from drug discovery through testing and FDA review, before a new drug is approved for use as a prescription medicine. The steps in the process are as follows:

- In vitro and animal testing.
- Proposal for human testing in clinical trials.
- Phase I clinical trials, to determine the drug's metabolism in the body and its most frequent side effects (typically involves 20 to 100 healthy individuals, or "subjects").
- Phase II clinical trials, to obtain preliminary data on whether the drug works in individuals with the disease or condition targeted by the drug (typically involves 30 to 500 individuals).
- Phase III clinical trials, to gather a larger set of data (typically involves several hundred to about 3,000 individuals).
- Formal request by the "drug sponsor" for the FDA to consider a drug for marketing approval; the drug sponsor, usually a pharmaceutical company (even if the drug was originally discovered in a university laboratory), files a new drug application.
- FDA scientists review the application to determine whether the studies described by the drug sponsor show that the drug is safe and effective for its proposed use.

U.S. Food and Drug Administration. "The FDA's Drug Review Process: Ensuring Drugs Are Safe and Effective," http://www.fda.gov/Drugs/ResourcesForYou/Consumers/ucm143475.htm (accessed June 17, 2010); "Inside Clinical Trials: Testing Medical Products in People," http://www.fda.gov/Drugs/ResourcesForYou/Consumers/ucm143531.htm (accessed October 1, 2010).

Table 7.4. Ongoing Clinical Trials with Approved and Investigative Cannabinoids

Agent(s)	Manufacturer	Condition	Administered form
Sativex	GW Pharmaceuticals	Bipolar affective disorder	oral spray
Smoked cannabis *vs.* Sativex	GW Pharmaceuticals	Multiple sclerosis	cigarette oral spray
Rimonabant (SR141716)	Sanofi-Aventis	Alcohol dependence	capsule
Marinol (dronabinol)	Abbott Laboratories	Anorexia nervosa	capsule
Cesamet (nabilone)	Valeant Pharmaceuticals	Pain associated with fibromyalgia Pain associated with diabetic neuropathy Pain associated with phantom limb neuropathy	capsule
SAB378 (with methadone)	Novartis Pharmaceuticals	Neuropathic (HIV-associated)	capsule
Sativex	GW Pharmaceuticals	Neuropathic (chemotherapy-induced)	oral spray
Rimonabant (SR141716)	Sanofi-Aventis	Weight gain (Prader-Willi syndrome)	capsule
Cannabidiol		Inflammatory bowel disease (Crohn's disease/ ulcerative colitis)	given as drops in olive oil
Cannabidiol		Cognitive dysfunction (Schizophrenia)	capsule
Marinol (dronabinol)	Abbott Laboratories	Cervical dystonia	capsule
		Opioid dependence	capsule (in combination with naltrexone)

Note: Sativex is a combination of tetrahydrocannabinol and cannabidiol; nabilone (Cesamet) is a synthetic analog of tetrahydrocannabinol; dronabinol (Marinol) is synthetic tetrahydrocannabinol.
Source: ClinicalTrials.gov. Accessed January 23, 2010.

(*continued from page 102*)
example, a randomized double-blind placebo-controlled trial to study the use of nabilone for sleep disturbances in patients with chronic pain (but not cancer pain) was recruiting participants in early 2010. The study investigators point out that some physicians prescribe nabilone to promote sleep in patients with chronic pain. One recently completed trial with **fibromyalgia** patients reported that nabilone was superior to the antidepressant amitriptyline (Elavil), which is known to improve sleep.[12]

WEIGHING THE SIDE EFFECTS

When used as a therapeutic agent to target a specific medical condition, marijuana or THC-containing products (plant-derived extracts or synthetic drugs) can have unintended, undesirable, or even unacceptable side effects. Ongoing toxicology and safety studies continue to examine the factors that influence the frequency of occurrence and severity of adverse effects of THC-containing drugs.

Concerns about possible adverse effects with long-term use of medical marijuana include drug dependence and, at the far end of the spectrum, the development of psychosis or psychotic episodes. Findings from neuropsychopharmacologic studies have provided support for a connection between cannabinoid receptor function in the brain and schizophrenia and other psychotic disorders, which suggests that cannabis use may play a role in schizophrenic and psychotic behaviors. In a study of healthy individuals with limited previous exposure to marijuana, the side effects of THC administered intravenously were limited to acute paranoia, panic, and hypotension. The blinded study evaluated two THC doses that were comparable to the THC content in marijuana joints.[13]

The health risks and concerns of medical marijuana administered by smoking argue for a thorough scientific analysis of short- and long-term side effects of smoked cannabis. Public health and medical experts have stated that they cannot ever promulgate the use of smoking for therapeutic purposes. Simply put, the inhalation of carcinogenic combustion products by smoking marijuana is hazardous to one's health. Nevertheless, in the absence of a therapy for a specific condition and with evidence of clinical benefit of smoked cannabis for a condition, such experts do recognize that its use should not be withheld. Numerous researchers in the public health and the medical and social sciences have pointed to the lack of studies with quantifiable toxicity data on smoked cannabis and the urgent need to obtain accurate safety data to help formulate evidence-based treatment and policy guidelines.[14]

The development or exacerbation of respiratory symptoms, such as acute or chronic bronchitis and obstructive lung disease, is a potential consequence of smoking marijuana. Marijuana smoke contains many of the same compounds found in tobacco smoke, notably carbon monoxide, cyanide, benzene, and hydrocarbons such as tar.[15] The range of respiratory symptoms can include persistent cough, wheezing or whistling chest sounds, shortness of breath while engaging in low-impact activities such as walking on level ground, coughing up phlegm in the morning, and tightness in the chest at night.[16]

Although long-term or heavy use of marijuana is associated with increased risk of cerebro- and cardiovascular events, such as stroke and cardiac arrest, there have been no reports of cerebro- or cardiotoxicity with oral formulations of synthetic THC (dronabinol and nabilone) or with the oromucosal spray of delta-9-tetrahydrocannabinol with cannabidiol in patients without a relevant medical history. However, exacerbation of cardiovascular disease is a potential side effect of smoking cannabis for therapeutic purposes, particularly if the patient has other risk factors (e.g., cigarette smoking, alcohol use, high cholesterol, hypertension, or obesity).

Most adverse events associated with THC-based products, as identified in controlled clinical trials, are not serious and none have been reported to be life-threatening. Dizziness has been cited as the most commonly reported side effect in the medical literature. In a systematic review of medical articles reporting clinical trial safety data on medical cannabinoid use (dronabinol or delta-9-tetrahydrocannabinol with cannabidiol) published between 1966 and 2007, no difference in the incidence of serious adverse events was found between cannabinoid-treated patients and untreated control patients.[17] The most commonly reported types of serious adverse events in clinical trial participants receiving cannabinoid treatment were relapse of multiple sclerosis (increase in frequency, duration, severity of muscle spasms), vomiting, and urinary tract infections. Clinical trial participants receiving either dronabinol or delta-9-tetrahydrocannabinol with cannabidiol had significantly greater occurrence of nonserious adverse events compared with the control groups.

Table 7.5. Adverse Events Associated with Dronabinol (Marinol) or delta-9-tetahydrocannabinol with cannabidiol (Sativex)	
• Shortness of breath, labored breathing	• Relapse of multiple sclerosis
• Pneumonia	• Convulsion
• Lower respiratory tract infection	• Dizziness
• Fluid accumulation in lungs	• Multiple sclerosis
• Vomiting	• Fever
• Diarrhea	• Mood alteration
• Abdominal pain	• Pain
• Constipation	• Urinary tract infection
• Gastroenteritis	• Blood in urine
• Duodenal ulcer	• Cervical cancer
• Progression of cancer	

Source: T. Wang et al., "Adverse Effects of Medial Cannabinoids: A Systematic Review," Canadian Medical Association Journal 178, 13 (June 2008): 1669–1678.

However, no difference in the incidence of nonserious adverse events was seen in delta-9-tetahydrocannabinol with cannabidiol-treated groups and control groups, suggesting that dronabinol has a less favorable toxicity profile. In observational studies (no control groups), serious and nonserious adverse events included relapse of multiple sclerosis, convulsion, dizziness, and mood alteration. Note that safety and toxicity reporting in clinical trials anticipate that nonserious adverse events reported will include those unrelated to the drug being investigated. Clinical trial data for the synthetic THC derivative nabilone were not included in the review, nor was smoked cannabis. Table 7.5 lists the array of serious and nonserious adverse events associated with the two medical cannabinoid products included in the analysis.

Researchers studying the effects of medical marijuana use, regardless of the route of administration, emphasize the need for longer-term toxicity data (i.e., safety data from studies evaluating long-term exposure) to further characterize the safety profile of individual products and medical marijuana in general. Importantly, the qualitative and quantitative toxicity and safety data collected for medical marijuana cannot be extrapolated to recreational use of marijuana for a number of reasons, including variations in the concentration of THC, dosage schedule and length of cumulative exposure, and the presence of coexisting medical conditions in patients.

LEGALITY OF MEDICAL MARIJUANA

In the United States, laws governing the cultivation, purchase, possession, and use of marijuana—the natural grown herbal product from *Cannabis sativa* plant—as medicine vary by state. As of December 2010, a total of 14 states and the District of Columbia allow the use of marijuana for medicinal purposes.

8

Current and Future Policy Trends on Marijuana Use

Brenda and Eddie were high-school sweethearts in Shasta County, California, about 150 miles north of Sacramento. They were also "pot-heads" with an entrepreneurial bent, who thought they could make a nice living growing marijuana in their sunny home state. They figured that with state and local government budgets tight, law enforcement resources would be focused on more serious crimes, like robbery and murder, than on busting pot growers. Besides, they reasoned, public sentiment favored the legalization of marijuana (an issue on the ballot every election year).

Having grown up in Shasta County, Brenda and Eddie knew the area well and found a secluded spot on a rural hillside surrounded by woods to start their pot farm. They did their research and they weren't afraid of work. In a short time, they planted 1,000 C. sativa plants that they got from friends who had backyard gardens and mini-farms of their own. Brenda and Eddie cleverly drew water from an uphill creek to fill a make-shift reservoir on the hillside that they lined with tarps and from which they ran hoses to water the plants. Everything was working according to plan and they were looking forward to reaping their first harvest.

However, in response to an anonymous tip, law enforcement officers made a raid on the farm as the sun rose one morning. In just a few short hours, three groups of officers had surrounded the farm, pulled up all the plants in the entire farm, and loaded them on flatbed trucks to be taken into the county's secure confiscated drug evidence building. Brenda and Eddie were arrested at their home that morning.

It could be argued that science is to blame for the renewed interest in decriminalizing or legalizing marijuana and for making its use more palatable to a larger segment of the general population. Certainly science has made great strides in uncovering the body's own THC (endogenous cannabinoids), the distribution of cannabinoid receptors in the central and peripheral nervous systems and in the immune system, the molecular pathways responsible for the production and degradation of THC and THC-like molecules, and the pathways leading to specific physiological changes following the binding of THC and THC-like molecules to cannabinoid receptors. Researchers continue to study the cannabinoid system for medical applications and for clues to understanding addictive behaviors and triggers and determinants of addiction at the molecular level. The interplay between the endocannabinoid, opioid, and dopamine systems in the brain suggest a biological basis for craving and dependence. Rather ironically, synthetic THC drugs are being evaluated in clinical trials as part of a drug combination treatment strategy to treat addiction to heroin and other opioids, and other substances of abuse. Another strategy being investigated is the use of drugs that block binding of the cannabinoid receptors (CB receptor antagonists) as a way to interfere with the dopamine reward pathway.

The medical use of marijuana should be regarded as a temporary or transitory situation until the health benefits of this ancient herb are harnessed into a smokeless medical product, such as a pill (already available). Scientists, clinicians, public health officials, and health advocates have communicated that they cannot promote smoking because of its harmful effects (smoking marijuana involves the inhalation of tar); however, these professionals acknowledge that smoking marijuana does provide benefits for specific conditions where no symptom relief is currently available and thus should be permitted.

From 1978 to the present, a total of 34 states in the United States have enacted laws that recognize the potential benefits of marijuana for medical purposes. Only 14 states and the District of Columbia allow the use of medical marijuana, including the growing of marijuana plants by those needing marijuana or their caretakers. (The other states have laws that allow research programs to grow and cultivate marijuana and evaluate its potential use in laboratory settings.) These state laws are inconsistent with federal law that prohibits the possession, use, distribution, and sale of marijuana and the cultivation and sale of marijuana plants. The U.S. Department of Justice announced in 2009 that the federal government will not prosecute cases involving the medical use of marijuana in states where medical marijuana laws exist.

THE MARIJUANA DEBATE TODAY

The marijuana debate today is really about the recreational use of marijuana: its potential for abuse (dependence and addiction), the collateral damage resulting from its use in settings such as driving and working while under the influence, and the collateral damage resulting from the international drug smuggling trade. Marijuana use and trafficking varies considerably by country. For example, while open cannabis cafés are found in the Netherlands, strict punitive laws exist in Mexico, the United States, and South Africa. Possession of small amounts of marijuana for either recreational or medicinal use is allowed or tolerated in the Netherlands, Spain, Belgium, and some regions of Switzerland. Pharmacies in the Netherlands became the first in Europe to sell pharmaceutical-grade cannabis (in 2003). In Canada, where marijuana use is illegal, one can apply to the Health Ministry of Canada (Health Canada) for a certificate of exemption to use marijuana for medical purposes. Health Canada sells the cannabis herb to patients if they do not want to grow it themselves.

In the United States, marijuana is "visible" in only 30% of states (those with medical marijuana laws), ranging from medical marijuana buyers clubs and clinics in California to pot dispensaries in Colorado to cannabis caravans in Montana to cannabis colleges in Michigan. Pot shops in states with medical marijuana laws sell hundreds of different varieties or strains of *C. sativa* plants and marijuana, all of which are available to be sniffed by potential customers who have the equivalent of a prescription. Californians, by and large, are accustomed to and accept the availability and common recreational use of marijuana. Not so in the conservative state of Oklahoma, which has the heaviest fines for marijuana possession in the country (up to $10,000).

U.S. policy on marijuana possession, use, and trafficking is not uniformly applied in all states and the District of Columbia. Policy makers, appointed

(*continues on page 114*)

MARIJUANA—A CASH CROP

A single marijuana plant that can yield approximately 32 ounces of marijuana is worth about $5,000, and could potentially bring a dealer almost $15,000 in sales of "dime bags" ($10 bags of less than a quarter of an ounce). Envision the value of the groves, fields, and even plantations of *C. sativa* plants grown on private and public woodlands . . . all of it illegal. Registered medical marijuana users in states with medical marijuana laws are allowed to grow a limited number of marijuana plants (except in Maryland and New Jersey) for personal medical use as clearly spelled out in the law. For example, registered users in Vermont are allowed a maximum of nine plants.

The federal government continues to dole out millions of antidrug dollars each year to state and local law enforcement agencies, including significant amounts earmarked for searching out and destroying marijuana farms. Drug-sniffing dogs are used, as are helicopters and small planes for aerial inspection of large swathes of wooded lands, in the pursuit of large-scale marijuana producers. As long as marijuana remains illegal, individuals involved in growing and cultivating marijuana without authorization are engaging in a criminal activity. In California, although there seems to be a certain level of tolerance with regard to recreational marijuana use, the laws are clear. In the northern California county of Mendocino, local law enforcers acknowledged that they are overwhelmed by the sheer number of illegal marijuana growers and therefore they target the large-scale producers.

"Marijuana, Inc.: Inside America's Pot Industry," a documentary produced and aired by CNBC in 2009, revealed some startling statistics about growing marijuana in Mendocino County:

- It is a more than billion-dollar-a-year industry, accounting for two-thirds of the local economy
- 60% of the population is involved in marijuana's growth and production
- Nationally the county is recognized as the number one producer of marijuana

Figure 8.1. Demonstrators protest a 2007 raid of a Los Angeles-area marijuana dispensary by federal agents. (*© Getty Images*)

Conflicting county, state, and federal laws aren't the challenge for law enforcement in Mendocino County; it's the number of growers, ranging from individuals with simple pot gardens in their backyards to entrepreneurs that gut and convert residential houses into hothouses overflowing with large, top-grade marijuana-producing plants. The blossoming growth of the marijuana crop industry in Mendocino has led to an increase in violent crimes–no wonder, considering the value of marijuana plants and the product. It's a potentially lucrative business, but also criminal. Would it all go away if marijuana were legalized? The question haunts almost everyone—health-care professionals, social scientists, policy makers, politicians, law enforcement professionals, teachers, and parents alike.

B. Kilmer et al., "Altered State? Assessing How Marijuana Legalization in California Could Influence Marijuana Consumption and Public Budgets," The Rand Corporation, http://www.rand.org/pubs/occasional_papers/2010/RAND_OP315.pdf (accessed September 30, 2010);
CNBC News, "Marijuana, Inc., Inside America's Pot Industry," January 22, 2009, http://www.cnbc.com/id/28281668/ (accessed September 30, 2010).

(*continued from page 111*)

and elected representatives, and the public continue to examine and question the best way to handle the marijuana trade. The black market (illegal underground sales and distribution) appears to be thriving, despite the risk of confiscation of money, investments, and product, despite the risk of jail or prison time and fines, despite the risk of violence associated with smuggling marijuana across borders. Violence and death are inseparable from the clashes between small-time and big-time drug dealers (including gangs and drug cartels) and law enforcement efforts.

Governments of the United States, Mexico, and several Central and South American countries are looking at the human lives lost and public funds spent fighting the marijuana trade as it currently exists. One thing is clear: all of the billions of dollars and all of the resources directed at eliminating or controlling marijuana cultivation and recreational use have not slowed down or curtailed the popularity, supply, or demand for this popular intoxicating substance. Policy makers and think tanks are weighing the potential benefits and pitfalls of legalizing and heavily taxing marijuana as a countermeasure to the ever-escalating drug trade and violence. It has been suggested that the scary, dangerous underworld of the drug business would be crippled if marijuana were simply legalized. According to a December 2009 article in the *Wall Street Journal,* marijuana accounts for as much as 65% of Mexican drug cartel revenues and helps fund their more profitable (and more risky) cocaine business operations. The Mexican drug cartels sell marijuana to U.S. dealers for cash and guns, and only recently has the Mexican border control implemented procedures for checking vehicles and persons coming into Mexico from the United States.

In the United States, arguments have been posed for legalizing marijuana as a means of increasing state revenues by imposing heavy taxes on marijuana at the point of sale. State and local revenues would also increase with lessened law enforcement resources and dollars spent on searching and tracking the possession and sale of marijuana. Legalization would also relieve overcrowding in jails and prisons. Proponents of legalizing and taxing marijuana cite ways in which a portion of the collected marijuana tax dollars could be allocated to programs for substance abuse prevention and treatment. According to a June 2010 article in the *New York Times,* proprietors of Colorado for-profit marijuana dispensaries are facing what all small-business owners face: the cost of licensing fees and the taxes on profits, plus the necessity of keeping abreast of and complying with state licensing regulations and various tax filings. The rest of the country is watching to see if the newly minted rules for medical marijuana businesses in Colorado can work in other states.

The decriminalization and legalization debates are likely to continue in a heated vein because of the concern and perception of marijuana as a gateway drug to "harder" drugs. As discussed in Chapter 1, study results examining whether or not marijuana use leads to the use of other more addictive and more harmful drugs are conflicting. Teen use of marijuana is of particular concern because it could set in motion a lifetime habit of chronic use, possibly pulling a teen into a drug culture that involves criminal behaviors, gangs, and violence. One question that seems to emerge in all discussions about legalizing marijuana: Is it more harmful that alcohol?

SUMMARY

A review of marijuana's use throughout history is eye-opening. Marijuana seems to have held a decidely prominent position in some religions, in medicine, in some ancient cultures, in artistic, intellectual, and monied circles in the West, and in the commercial trade world through World War II. Today, marijuana seems to have resumed its position on center stage, which is largely attributable to the public's recognition of the medical and commercial benefits of *C. sativa* (including the use of hemp in cloth). The recreational use of marijuana will likely be studied and debated by social scientists, public health researchers, social scientists, epidemiologists, biomedical researchers, health care professionals, and policy makers for years to come.

Notes

Chapter 1

1. E.B. Russo et al., "Phytochemical and Genetic Analyses of Ancient Cannabis from Central Asia," *Journal of Experimental Botany* 59, 15 (November 2008): 4171–4182.

2. United Nations, "Report of the International Narcotics Control Board for 2009," http://www.incb.org/incb/en/annual-report-2009.html (accessed March 5, 2010).

3. L. Degenhardt et al., "Toward a Global View of Alcohol, Tobacco, Cannabis, and Cocaine Use: Findings from the WHO World Mental Health Surveys," *Public Library of Science Medicine* 5, 7 (July 2008): e141.

4. United Nations Office on Drugs and Crime, *World Drug Report 2009,* http://www.unodc.org/unodc/en/data-and-analysis/WDR-2009.html (accessed March 5, 2010).

5. A. Agrawal and M.T. Lynskey, "Tobacco and Cannabis Co-occurrence: Does Route of Administration Matter?" *Drug and Alcohol Dependency* 99, 1–3 (January 2009): 240–247.

6. H. Kalant, "Medicinal Use of Cannabis: History and Current Status," *Pain Research Management* 6, 2 (Summer 2001): 80–91.

7. S.A. Ahmed et al., "Structure Determination and Absolute Configuration of Cannabichromanone Derivatives from High Potency *Cannabis sativa,*" *Tetrahedron Letters* 49, 42 (October 2008): 6050–6053.

8. A.C. Howlett et al., "Cannabinoid Physiology and Pharmacology: 30 Years of Progress," *Neuropharmacology* 47, supplement 1 (2004): 345–358.

9. Kalant, "Medicinal Use of Cannabis;" G. Andrews and S. Vinkenoog, eds., "Introduction" in *The Book of Grass: An Anthology of Indian Hemp* (New York: Grove Press, 1967).

10. C.H. Ashton, "Pharmacology and Effects of Cannabis: A Brief Review," *British Journal of Psychiatry* 178, 2 (February 2001): 101–106.

11. Kalant, "Medicinal Use of Cannabis."

12. S. Jayanthi et al., "Heavy Marijuana Users Show Increased Serum Apolipoprotein CIII Levels: Evidence from Proteomic Analyses," *Molecular Psychiatry* 15, 1 (January 2010): 101–112.

13. H. Kalant, "Adverse Effects of Cannabis on Health: An Update of the Literature since 1996," *Progress in Neuro-Psychopharmacology and Biological Psychiatry* 28, 5 (August 2004): 849–863; F. Grotenhermen, "The Toxicology of Cannabis and Cannabis Prohibition," *Chemistry and Biodiversity* 4, 8 (August 2007): 1744–1769; N. Wilson and J.L. Cadet, "Comorbid Mood, Psychosis, and Marijuana Abuse Disorders: A Theoretical Review," *Journal of Addiction Diseases* 28, 4 (October 2009): 309–319; M. Yücel et al., "Regional Brain Abnormalities Associated with Long-term Heavy Cannabis Use," *Archives of General Psychiatry* 65, 6 (June 2008): 694–701; and T.H. Moore et al., "Cannabis Use and Risk of Psychotic or Affective Mental Health Outcomes: A Systematic Review," *Lancet* 370, 9584 (July 2007): 319–328.

14. M. Cohen, N. Solowij, and V. Carr, "Cannabis, Cannabinoids and Schizophrenia: Integration of the Evidence," *Australian and New Zealand Journal of Psychiatry* 42, 5 (May 2008): 357–368.

15. H. Kalant, "Adverse Effects of Cannabis on Health: An Update of the Literature since 1996," *Progress in Neuro-Psychopharmacology and Biological Psychiatry* 28, 5 (August 2004): 849–863; F. Grotenhermen, "The Toxicology of Cannabis and Cannabis Prohibition," *Chemistry and Biodiversity* 4, 8 (August 2007): 1744–1769; C.Y. Chen and K.M. Lin, "Health Consequences of Illegal Drug Use," *Current Opinions in Psychiatry* 22, 3 (May 2009): 287–292.

16. H. Kalant, "Adverse Effects of Cannabis on Health: An Update of the Literature since 1996," *Progress in Neuro-Psychopharmacology and Biological Psychiatry* 28, 5 (August 2004): 849–863.

17. R.E. Tarter et al., "Predictors of Marijuana Use in Adolescents Before and After Licit Drug Use: Examination of the Gateway Hypothesis," *American Journal of Psychiatry* 163, 12 (December 2006): 2134–2140.

18. J.E. Joy, S.J. Watson, Jr., J.A. Bensons, Jr., eds., *Marijuana and Medicine: Assessing the Science Base* (Washington, D.C.: National Academy Press, 1999).

Chapter 2

1. Russo et al., "Phytochemical and Genetic Analyses of Ancient Cannabis from Central Asia,"
2. R. Rudgley, "Cannabis," in *The Encyclopedia of Psychoactive Substances* (New York: Thomas Dunne Books, 1998), http://www.cannabis.net/hist/index.html (accessed October 1, 2010); E. Russo, "Cannabis in India: Ancient lore and modern medicine," in *Cannabinoids as Therapeutics,* ed. Raphael Mechoulam (Switzerland: Birkhäuser Verlag, 2005).
3. Ibid.
4. Kalant, "Medicinal Use of Cannabis."
5. E.L. Abel, *Marihuana: The First Twelve Thousand Years* (New York: Plenum Press, 1980).
6. C. Kolosov, "Evaluating the Public Interest: Regulation of Industrial Hemp Under the Controlled Substances Act," *UCLA Law Review* 57, 1 (October 2009): 237–274, http:/UCLAlawreview.org/pdf/57-1-5.pdf.

7. A.W. Zuardi, "History of *Cannabis* as a Medicine: A Review," *Revisita Brasileira de Psiquiatria* 28, 2 (June 2006): 153–157; D.E. Moerman, *Medicinal Plants of Native America* (Ann Arbor: Museum of Anthropology, University of Michigan, 1986).
8. Zuardi, "History of *Cannabis* as a Medicine."
9. Kolosov, "Evaluating the Public Interest: Regulation of Industrial Hemp."
10. L. Grinspoon and J. Bakalar, *Marihuana: The Forbidden Medicine* (New York: Yale University Press, 1993).
11. Abel, *Marihuana: The First Twelve Thousand Years.*
12. Zuardi, "History of *Cannabis* as a Medicine."
13. Abel, *Marihuana: The First Twelve Thousand Years.*
14. Zuardi, "History of *Cannabis* as a Medicine."

Chapter 3

1. Ashton, "Pharmacology and Effects of Cannabis;" R.A. Hirst, D.G. Lambert, and W.G. Notcutt, "Pharmacology and Potential Therapeutic Uses of Cannabis," *British Journal of Anaesthesia* 81, 1 (July 1998): 77–84.
2. Howlett et al., "Cannabinoid Physiology and Pharmacology;"

R.A. Hirst, D.G. Lambert, and W.G. Notcutt, "Pharmacology and Potential Therapeutic Uses of Cannabis," *British Journal of Anaesthesia* 81, 1 (July 1998): 77–84.

3. Ashton, "Pharmacology and Effects of Cannabis."

4. F. Grotenhermen, "Pharmacology of Cannabinoids," *Neuro Endocrinology Letters* 25, 1–2 (February–April 2004): 14–23.

5. R.A. Hirst, D.G. Lambert, and W.G. Notcutt, "Pharmacology and Potential Therapeutic Uses of Cannabis," *British Journal of Anaesthesia* 81, 1 (July 1998): 77–84; R.G. Pertwee, "Cannabinoid Pharmacology: The First 66 Years," *British Journal of Pharmacology* 147, supplement 1 (January 2006): S163–S171.

6. A.C. Howlett et al., "International Union of Pharmacology. XXVII. Classification of cannabinoid receptors," *Pharmacological Reviews* 54, 2 (June 2002): 161–202.

7. A.J. Brown, "Novel Cannabinoid Receptors," *British Journal of Pharmacology* 152, 5 (November 2007): 567–575; F.R. de Fonseca et al., "The Endocannabinoid System: Physiology and Pharmacology," *Alcohol and Alcoholism* 40, 1 (January–February 2005): 2–14.

8. P. Pacher, S. Batkai, and G. Kunos, "The Endocannabinoid System as an Emerging Target of Pharmacotherapy," *Pharmacological Reviews* 58, 3 (2006): 389–462.

9. M. Yücel et al., "Regional Brain Abnormalities Associated with Long-term Heavy Cannabis Use," *Archives of General Psychiatry* 65, 6 (June 2008): 694–701; A.C. Howlett et al., "International Union of Pharmacology. XXVII. Classification of Cannabinoid Receptors," *Pharmacological Reviews* 54, 2 (June 2002): 161–202.

10. R.G. Pertwee, "The Diverse CB1 and CB2 Receptor Pharmacology of Three Plant Cannabinoids: Δ^9-tetrahydrocannabinol, cannabidiol and Δ^9-tetrahydrocannabivarin," *British Journal of Pharmacology* 153, 2 (January 2008): 199–215.

11. G.A. Cabral and A. Staab, "Effects on the Immune System," *Handbook of Experimental Pharmacology* 168 (2005): 385–423.

12. Pertwee, "The Diverse CB1 and CB2 Receptor Pharmacology of Three Plant Cannabinoids."

13. R.G. Pertwee, "The Therapeutic Potential of Drugs That Target the Cannabinoid Receptors or Modulate the Tissue Levels or

Actions of Endocannabinoids," *The AAPS Journal* 7, 3 (October 2005): E625–E654.

14. R.G. Pertwee, "Cannabinoid Pharmacology: The First 66 Years," *British Journal of Pharmacology* 147, supplement 1 (January 2006): S163–S171.

15. Ibid.

16. D. C. D'Souza et al., "The Psychotomimetic Effects of Intravenous Delta-9- tetra-hydrocannabinol in Healthy Individuals: Implications for Psychosis," *Neuropsychopharmacology* 29, 8 (August 2004): 1558–1572.

17. F. Grotenhermen, "Pharmacokinetics and Pharmacodynamics of Cannabinoids," *Clinical Pharmacokinetics* 4, 12 (December 2003): 2367–2377.

18. C.R. Craig and R.E. Stitzel, eds., *Modern Pharmacology along with Clinical Applications.* 6th ed. (Baltimore: Lippincott Williams & Wilkins, 2003).

19. M.A. Heustis, "Human Cannabinoid Pharmacokinetics," *Chemistry and Biodiversity* 4, 8 (August 2007): 1770–1804.

20. Ibid.

21. Ibid.

22. Craig and Stitzel, *Modern Pharmacology along with Clinical Applications.*

23. Kalant, "Medicinal Use of Cannabis."

24. Craig and Stitzel, *Modern Pharmacology along with Clinical Applications.*

25. Grotenhermen, "Pharmacokinetics and Pharmacodynamics of Cannabinoids;" Heustis, "Human Cannabinoid Pharmacokinetics," *Chemistry and Biodiversity* 4, 8 (August 2007): 1770–1804.

26. C. Sachse-Seeboth et al., "Interindividual Variation in the Pharmacokinetics of Delta9-tetrahydrocannabinol as Related to Genetic Polymorphisms in CYP2C9," *Clinical Pharmacology and Therapeutics* 85, 3 (March 2009): 273–276.

Chapter 4

1. L. Degenhardt et al., "Toward a Global View of Alcohol, Tobacco, Cannabis, and Cocaine Use: Findings from the WHO World Mental Health Surveys," *Public Library of Science Medicine* 5, 7 (July 2008): e141.

2. L.D. Johnston, P.M. O'Malley, J.G. Bachman, and J.E. Schulenberg, *Monitoring the Future: National Survey Results on Drug Use, 1975–2008*: Volume I: "Secondary School Students," http://monitoringthefuture.org/pubs.html (accessed February 25, 2010); Substance Abuse and Mental Health Services

Administration, *Results from the 2008 National Survey on Drug Use and Health: National Findings*, Office of Applied Studies, NSDUH Series H-36, HHS Publication No. (SMA) 09-4434 (Rockville, Md.: September 2009).

3. Substance Abuse and Mental Health Services Administration (SAMHSA), *Results from the 2008 National Survey on Drug Use and Health: National Findings*, Office of Applied Studies, NSDUH Series H-36, HHS Publication No. (SMA) 09-4434 (Rockville, Md.: September 2009).

4. Ibid.

5. National Institute on Drug Abuse, "Highlights of the 2009 *Monitoring the Future* Survey," http://www.cadca.org/files/resources/MTF_TwoPager_2009_.pdf (accessed February 25, 2010).

6. SAMHSA, *Results from the 2008 National Survey on Drug Use and Health*.

7. Substance Abuse and Mental Health Services Administration, Office of Applied Studies. "Treatment Episode Data Set (TEDS): 1997–2007," National Admissions to Substance Abuse Treatment Services, DASIS Series: S-47, http://www.oas.samhsa.gov/copies.

cfm (accessed February 25, 2010).

Chapter 5

1. A. Elkashef et al., "Marijuana Neurobiology and Treatment," *Substance Abuse* 29, 3 (2008): 17–29; SAMHSA, *Results from the 2008 National Survey on Drug Use and Health;* A. Elkashef et al., "Marijuana Neurobiology and Treatment," *Substance Abuse* 29, 3 (2008): 17–29.

2. A.W. Graham et al., eds., *Principles of Addiction Medicine*. 3d ed. (Chevy Chase, Md.: American Society of Addiction Medicine, Inc., 2003).

3. M.H. Beers et al., eds., *The Merck Manual of Diagnosis and Therapy*. 18th ed. (Whitehouse Station, N.J.: Merck Research Laboratories, 2006).

4. Ibid.

5. Merck Sharp & Dohme Corp., "Marijuana (Cannabis): Drug Use and Dependence," in *Merck Manual, Professional Edition*.

6. Substance Abuse and Mental Health Services Administration, "Treatment Episode Data Set (TEDS): 1997–2007," National Admissions to Substance Abuse Treatment Services, DASIS Series: S-47, http://www.oas.samhsa.gov/

copies.cfm (accessed February 25, 2010).

7. SAMHSA, *Results from the 2008 National Survey on Drug Use and Health.*

8. A. Elkashef et al., "Marijuana Neurobiology and Treatment," *Substance Abuse* 29, 3 (2008): 17–29; I.D. Montoya and F. Vocci, "Novel Medications to Treat Addictive Disorders," *Current Psychiatry Reports* 10, 5 (October 2008): 392–398.

9. Elkashef et al., "Marijuana Neurobiology and Treatment."

10. National Institute on Drug Abuse, "Medications Development for the Treatment of Cannabis-Related Disorders (R01)," http://grants.nih.gov/grants/guide/pa-files/PA-07-365.html (accessed October 1, 2010).

11. A.D. Hathaway et al., "Cannabis Dependence as a Primary Drug Use-Related Problem: The Case for Harm Reduction-Oriented Treatment Options," *Substance Use and Misuse* 44, 7 (2009): 990–1008.

12. K.L. Steinberg et al., *Brief Counseling for Marijuana Dependence: A Manual for Treating Adults,* Substance Abuse and Mental Health Services Administration, DHHS Publication No. (SMA) 05-402 (Rockville, Md.: Center for Substance Abuse Treatment, 2005).

13. C. Stanger et al., "A Randomized Trial of Contingency Management for Adolescent Marijuana Abuse and Dependence," *Drug and Alcohol Dependency* 105, 3 (December 2009): 240–247.

14. E. Bernstein, "Screening and Brief Intervention to Reduce Marijuana Use Among Youth and Young Adults in a Pediatric Emergency Department," *Academic Emergency Medicine* 16, 11 (November 2009): 1174–1185.

15. See note 10; I.D. Montoya and F. Vocci, "Novel Medications to Treat Addictive Disorders," *Current Psychiatry Reports* 10, 5 (October 2008): 392–398.

16. J.R. Clapper, R.A. Mangieri, and D. Piomelli, "The Endocannabinoid System as a Target for the Treatment of Cannabis Dependence," *Neuropharmacology* 56, supplement 1 (2009): 235–243.

17. A.J. Budney, R. Roffman, R.S. Stephens, and D. Walker, "Marijuana Dependence and its Treatment," *Addiction Science and Clinical Practice* 4, 1 (December 2007): 4–16; F.R. Levin and H.D. Kleber, "Use of Dronabinol for Cannabis Dependence: Two

Case Reports and Review," *American Journal of Addiction* 17, 2 (March–April 2008): 161–164.

18. M. Haney et al., "Effects of THC and Lofexidine in a Human Laboratory Model of Marijuana Withdrawal and Relapse," *Psychopharmacology* 197 (March 2008): 157–168.

19. Clapper, Mangieri, and Piomelli, "The Endocannabinoid System as a Target for the Treatment of Cannabis Dependence."

20. Elkashef et al., "Marijuana Neurobiology and Treatment."

21. National Institute on Drug Abuse, "Marijuana: An Update from the National Institute on Drug Abuse," November 2009, http://www.drugabuse.gov/tib/marijuana.html (accessed February 20, 2010).

Chapter 6

1. E.M. Brecher, "The Consumer Union Report—Licit and Illicit Drugs," http://www.druglibrary.org/schaffer/LIBRARY/studies/cu/cumenu.htm (accessed January 12, 2010).

2. U.S. Drug Enforcement Administration, "Chapter 1: The Controlled Substances Act," http://www.justice.gov/dea/pubs/abuse/1-csa.htm (accessed February 22, 2010).

3. Ibid.

4. Office of Diversion Control, U.S. Department of Justice, Drug Enforcement Administration, "Controlled Substances Schedules," http://www.deadiversion.usdoj.gov (accessed October 1, 2010).

5. Office of National Drug Control Policy, "Who's Really in Prison for Marijuana?" 2005, http:// http://www.ncjrs.gov/ondcppubs/publications/pdf/whos_in_prison_for_marij.pdf (accessed January 12, 2010).

6. Americans for Safe Access, "Federal Marijuana Law," http://www.safeaccessnow.org/article.php?id=2638 (accessed March 1, 2010); National Public Radio, "Medical Marijuana Arrests; Calif. Isn't Mellow Yet." September 19, 2009, http://www.npr.org/templates/story/story.php?storyId=112961966 (accessed September 24, 2010).

7. U.S. Federal Bureau of Investigation, "2008 Crime in the United States, http://www.fbi.gov/ucr/cius2008/arrests/index.html (accessed February 28, 2010).

8. Office of National Drug Control Policy, "Marijuana Facts and Figures," http://www.whitehousedrugpolicy.gov/drugfact/marijuana/

marijuana_ff.html#arrests (accessed January 12, 2010).

9. R.S. King and M. Mauer, "The War on Marijuana: The Transformation of the War on Drugs in the 1990s," *Harm Reduction Journal* 3, 6 (February 2006).

10. Office of National Drug Control Policy, "Who's Really in Prison for Marijuana?" 2005, http:// http://www.ncjrs.gov/ondcppubs/publications/pdf/whos_in_prison_for_marij.pdf (accessed January 12, 2010).

Chapter 7

1. Zuardi, "History of *Cannabis* as a Medicine;" T. Geller, "Cannabinoids: A Secret History," *Chemical Heritage Magazine* 25, 2 (Summer 2007), https://chemicalheritage.org/pubs/ch-v25n2-articles/feature_cannabinoids.html (accessed January 5, 2010).

2. Zuardi, "History of *Cannabis* as a Medicine;" T. Geller, "Cannabinoids: A Secret History;" R.D. Hosking and J.P. Zajicek, "Therapeutic Potential of Cannabis in Pain Medicine," *British Journal of Anaesthesiology* 101, 1 (July 2008): 59–68.

3. E. Russo, "Cognoscenti of Cannabis I: Jacques-Joseph Moreau (1804–1884)," *Journal*

of *Cannabis Therapeutics* 1, 1 (2001): 85–88.

4. Abel, *Marihuana: The First Twelve Thousand Years.*

5. M. Aldrich, "History of Therapeutic Cannabis," in *Cannabis in Medical Practice* (Jefferson, N.C.: McFarland, 1997).

6. R.D. Hosking and J.P. Zajicek, "Therapeutic Potential of Cannabis in Pain Medicine," *British Journal of Anaesthesiology* 101, 1 (July 2008): 59–68; G.F. Phillips, "Analytical and Legislative Aspects of Cannabis," in *Cannabis: The genus Cannabis* (Amsterdam: Harwood Academic Publishers, 1998), 71–114.

7. D.I. Abrams, "Vaporization as a Smokeless Cannabis Delivery System: A Pilot Study," *Clinical Pharmacology and Therapeutics* 82, 5 (November 2007): 572–578.

8. GW Pharmaceuticals, "Cultivation: Breeding Programme," http://www.gwpharm.com/cultivation.aspx (accessed October 1, 2010).

9. U.S. National Institutes of Health, "Randomized Placebo-Controlled Crossover Trial With THC (Delta 9-Tetrahydrocannabinol) for the Treatment of Cramps in Amyotrophic Lateral Sclerosis," http://clinicaltrials.

gov/ct2/show/study/ NCT00812851 (accessed March 1, 2010).

10. U.S. National Institutes of Health, "Dronabinol Naltrexone Treatment for Opioid Dependence," http:// clinicaltrials.gov/ct2/show/ NCT01024335 (accessed March 1, 2010).

11. W. Gonsiorek et al., "Sch35966 Is a Potent, Selective Agonist at the Peripheral Cannabinoid Receptor (CB2) in Rodents and Primates," *British Journal of Pharmacology* 151 (2007): 1262–1271; M. Ibrahim et al., "Activation of CB2 Cannabinoid Receptors by AM1241 Inhibits Experimental Neuropathic Pain: Pain Inhibition by Receptors Not Present in the CNS," *Proceedings of the National Academy of Sciences of the United States of America* 100, 18 (September 2, 2003): 10529-33; B. Le Foll and S.R. Goldberg, "Cannabinoid CB1 Receptor Antagonists as Promising New Medications for Drug Dependence," *The Journal of Pharmacology and Experimental Therapeutics* 312, 3 (March 2005): 875-883; P. Pacher, S. Batkai, and G. Kunos, "The Endocannabinoid System as an Emerging Target of Pharmacotherapy," *Pharmacological Reviews* 58, 3 (2006): 389–462; B. Szabo, "Pharmacology of Cannabinoid Receptors." *Biotrend Reviews* 2, 2 (2008): 1-14; B.B. Yao et al., "In Vitro Pharmacological Characterization of AM1241: A Protean Agonist at the Cannabinoid CB2 Receptor?" *British Journal of Pharmacology* 149, 2 (September 2006): 145-154.

12. U.S. National Institutes of Health, "Use of the Cannabinoid Nabilone for the Promotion of Sleep in Chronic, Non-malignant Pain Patients," http://clinicaltrials.gov/ct2/ show/NCT00384410 (accessed March 1, 2010); M.A. Ware, M.A. Fitzcharles, L. Joseph, and Y. Shir, "The Effects of Nabilone on Sleep in Fibromyalgia: Results of a Randomized Controlled Trial," *Anesthesia and Analgesia* 110, 2 (February 2010): 604–610.

13. D.C. D'Souza et al., "The Psychotomimetic Effects of Intravenous Delta-9-tetrahydrocannabinol in Healthy Individuals: Implications for Psychosis," *Neuropsychopharmacology* 29, 8 (August 2004): 1558–1572.

14. J.E. Joy, S.J. Watson, Jr., J.A. Bensons, Jr., eds., *Marijuana and Medicine: Assessing the Sci-*

ence Base (Washington, D.C.: National Academy Press, 1999).

15. S. Aldington et al., "Effects of Cannabis on Pulmonary Structure, Function and Symptoms," *Thorax* 62, 12 (December 2007): 1058–1063; P. Lange, "Cannabis and the Lung," *Thorax* 62, 12 (December 2007): 1036–1037.

16. J.M. Tetrault et al., "Effects of Marijuana Smoking on Pulmonary Function and Respiratory Complications: A Systematic Review," *Archives of Internal Medicine*, 167, 3 (February 2007): 221–228.

17. T. Wang, J-P. Collet, S. Shapiro, and M.A. Ware, "Adverse Effects of Medical Cannabinoids: A Systematic Review," *Canadian Medical Association Journal* 178, 13 (June 2008): 1669–1678.

Glossary

addiction   A set of behaviors characterized by compulsive use of a psychoactive (mind-altering) drug or substance and a compulsion to obtain more for personal use.

agonists   Molecules that bind to a receptor and produce an effect or response. In pharmacology, drugs may be characterized as agonists if they act by binding to a receptor.

Alzheimer's disease   A progressive degenerative disease of the brain marked by memory impairment, personality changes, and loss of intellectual function. Onset may occur at any age, although this disease was originally dubbed *presenile dementia* because it was generally seen in persons under 65 years of age. (*Senile dementia* refers to mental deterioration due to the aging process.)

analgesia   Relief from pain or the deadening of the sensation of pain

antagonists   Molecules that bind to a receptor without producing an effect or response. Upon binding to a receptor, antagonists block the binding of agonists to that receptor, thereby preventing or inhibiting an action or response.

antiemesis   The prevention of nausea and vomiting. Antiemetic drugs prevent or alleviate nausea and vomiting.

atherosclerosis   A chronic inflammatory disease marked by the thickening of the wall of the arteries due to the buildup of cholesterol and lipids (fats) or plaques.

autoimmunity   A condition in which the body mounts specific humoral and cell-mediated immune responses against its own tissue(s).

autonomic nervous system   The motor nerves of the peripheral nervous system that carry signals to smooth muscle, cardiac muscles, and glands (endocrine organs).

beriberi   A dietary disease caused by vitamin B1 (thiamin) deficiency and characterized by inflammation of the peripheral nerves, changes in structure and function of the heart, and swelling of the tissues due to abnormal fluid accumulation. Historically common in China, Japan, and other Asian countries where rice is a food staple.

bronchodilation   An increase in the diameter of the large air passages of the lungs (bronchi), thereby allowing more air to enter the lungs

cachexia   A state of general ill health, physical wasting, and malnutrition

cannabinoids   A group of more that 60 chemical compounds found in the *Cannabis sativa* plant, the most abundant of which is delta-9-tetrahydro-cannabinol (i.e., tetrahydrocannabinol, or THC). There are three classes of cannabinoids: the plant-derived phytocannabinoids, endogenous cannabinoids produced by the body, and synthetic cannabinoids that are made in the laboratory. All are chemically similar and have similar activities.

catalepsy   A trancelike state characterized by the loss of voluntary motion; a body posture that is fixed and maintained for a prolonged period of time, giving the appearance of being immobilized

cell-mediated immunity   The body's immune response (defense system) against infection and foreign substances that is mediated by specialized immune system cells (T lymphocytes or T cells)

central nervous system   In humans and higher animals, the part of the nervous system that consists of the brain and spinal cord. Generally contrasted with the peripheral nervous system.

craving   An intense, urgent, or abnormal desire or longing for a rewarding object or experience

cytochrome P450 system   The family of enzymes responsible for the metabolism of some foods and beverages and many medications as well as recreational drugs, including THC

dependence   Drug dependence can be physical or psychological or both. Physical dependence is a biological response that reflects a disturbance of the body's natural balance (equilibrium or homeostatic mechanism) due to repeated or chronic exposure to a substance such as alcohol or another drug. Psychological dependence, distinct from physical dependence, is the intense desire or craving to repeatedly use a drug or obtain a drug and is a component of addictive behavior.

dosage   The size, frequency, and the number of doses administered

dysentery   A disorder affecting the bowels caused by microbes or chemical irritants, characterized by the inflammation of the intestines and associated with abdominal pain and frequent stools containing blood and mucus.

dysphoria   An exaggerated feeling of agitation, restlessness, and unhappiness; it is derived from the Greek word meaning "hard to bear." Marijuana and other drugs, including alcohol, may induce this feeling.

endocannabinoids   See *endogenous cannabinoids*.

endogenous cannabinoids . Cannabinoids that are produced by the body (e.g., anandamide and 2-arachidonoylglycerol), as opposed to cannabinoid compounds extracted from the *Cannabis sativa* plant. The body's natural cannabinoids are produced and released by neurons in the central and peripheral nervous systems.

endothelial cells   Specialized cells that line the inner surface of blood vessels

euphoria   An exaggerated feeling of physical and mental well-being. Marijuana, and other drugs, including alcohol, may induce this feeling.

fatty acid   An organic molecule that is made up of a long, unbranched, single chain of carbon atoms containing one or more double bonds. Fatty acids are found in triglycerides, the most common form of fat (a concentrated source of energy) in our bodies.

fibromyalgia   Pain and stiffness in the muscles and joints

glaucoma   A disease of the eye characterized by increased pressure in the eye (intraocular pressure) that damages the optic nerve, affecting vision

gout   A disorder typically characterized by deposits of crystals of uric acid in and around the joints of the hands and feet that can lead to crippling destruction of the joints or recurring arthritis. Uric acid buildup is due to abnormal metabolism of nitrogen-containing compounds called purines that are found naturally in foods and that are components of DNA and RNA molecules (the genetic materials, deoxyribonucleic acid and ribonucleic acid).

humoral immunity   The body's immune response (defense system) against infection and foreign substances that is mediated by antibodies or immunoglobulins, which are produced by the B cells of the immune system.

hypertension   Abnormally high blood pressure that usually has no symptoms and can be due to underlying disease or the use of certain drugs.

Uncontrolled high blood pressure increases the risk of serious health problems, such as heart attack and stroke.

hypotension   Abnormally low blood pressure that can cause fainting and dizziness. Low blood pressure can be caused by dehydration, or by abnormal signals from brain to the heart. Severely low blood pressure can lead to shock, a life-threatening condition in which the brain and other vital organs are deprived of oxygen and nutrients.

in vitro   Within a test tube or other artificial environment

in vivo   Within a living body or organism

ligand   A small molecule that binds to a larger (receptor) molecule

multiple sclerosis   A degenerative disease of the central nervous system that is characterized by weakness, tremors, and lack of coordination

mycobacteria   A family of bacteria found in soil, water, and dairy products; in animals and humans, these bacteria are parasitic and cause disease, including the species that cause tuberculosis and leprosy.

narcotic   Derived from the Greek word meaning "to numb," as in to dull the senses, lull, or induce sleep. Any drug or substance that produces a generalized depression of brain functioning, which manifests as insensibility or stupor. The legal and regulatory use of the word refers to restricted or controlled distribution, sale, and use.

neuron   Also called a *nerve cell*. Neurons are specialized cells of the nervous system that relay information to and from the brain and spinal cord. Neurons communicate with each other and with target cells of muscles and glands (endocrine organs) through electrochemical signalling.

neuropathic pain   The pain that results from the stimulation of nerve cells in the central or peripheral nervous system and that is commonly felt as tingling or burning

neurotransmitters   The chemical substances released from neurons (specialized cells of the nervous system) upon electrical stimulation; communication between neurons occurs when electric impulses trigger the release and uptake of neurotransmitters in these cells.

peripheral nervous system   The nervous system outside of the brain and spinal cord. The peripheral nervous system consists of the sensory and motor nerves that carry signals into and out of the central nervous system.

pharmacodynamics   The branch of pharmacology that describes the physiological, molecular, and biochemical effects of drugs on the body

pharmacokinetics   The branch of pharmacology that describes the fate and activity of drugs in the body over time, including the processes of drug absorption, distribution, metabolism, and elimination.

phytocannabinoids   Cannabinoid compounds found in the *Cannabis sativa* plant

psychoactive   Affecting the mind (conscious and unconscious mental processing) and behavior; synonymous with *psychotropic*. Psychoactive drugs act on the central nervous system and are capable of modifying mental (cognitive) activity and/or the behaviors of an individual. The root of the word is derived from the Greek *psyche*, meaning *life* or *soul*), generally regarded as the organ of thought and judgment.

receptor biology   The study of the molecules on the surface of cells (receptors) that bind highly specific extracellular signaling molecules (ligands), triggering a set of cellular, molecular, and biochemical events that produce a response. The psychoactive effects of marijuana are caused by the binding of THC, the major chemical compound in *Cannabis sativa*, to cannabinoid receptors in the brain.

solubility   The ability of a substance or drug to be dissolved. In pharmacology, a drug's solubility is generally qualified as either aqueous (in water) or lipid (in fat-containing liquid) solubility.

spasticity   Awkward movement resulting from muscle stiffness due to damage of the part of the brain that controls voluntary movement or damage to the nerves traveling from the brain down to the spinal cord

synaptic vesicles   Small membrane-bound structures found in neurons (nerve cells) near the synapse or the junction between two adjacent neurons. Synaptic vesicles contain neurotransmitters, and when a neuron is stimulated, the synaptic vesicles fuse with the cell membrane, releasing neurotransmitters into the synapse.

tachycardia   An increased or excessively rapid heartbeat (rate)

THC   Tetrahydrocannabinol or delta-9-tetrahydrocannabinol: the most abundant and the most psychoactive cannabinoid compound in the *C. sativa* plant

tolerance   A biological phenomenon in which there is a decrease or loss of effectiveness of a specific dose of a substance with repeated or prolonged use. An increase in dose is required to produce the same effect that a smaller dose produced originally.

transdermal   To enter the body through the skin. Transdermal drugs are typcially administered as a patch applied to the skin.

withdrawal   A biological response that describes the body's reaction to no longer having a specific drug or substance in its system (the adaptation of the brain and the rest of the body to the drug's absence). The physiological symptoms of withdrawal, which emerge when substance use is abruptly stopped, are generally unique to the classes of drugs.

further Resources

Books

Abel, Earnest L. *Marihuana: The First Twelve Thousand Years.* New York: Plenum Press, 1980.

Brill, H., and G.G. Nahas. "Cannabis Intoxication and Mental Illness." In: *Marihuana in Science and Medicine,* ed. G.G. Nahas. New York: Raven Press; 1984, 263–306.

Castle, D., and R.Murray, eds. *Marijuana and Madness: Psychiatry and Neurobiology.* Cambridge: Cambridge University Press, 2004.

Chapkins, W., and R.J. Webb. *Dying to Get High: Marijuana as Medicine.* New York: New York University Press, 2008.

ElSohly, M.A., ed. *Marijuana and the Cannabinoids.* Totowa, N.J.: Humana Press, 2007.

Guy, Geoffrey, Brian Whittle, and Philip J. Robson, eds. *The Medicinal Use of Cannabis.* London: Royal Society of Pharmacists, 2004.

Mikuriya, Tod H., ed. *Marijuana Medical Papers: 1839–1972.* Berkeley, Calif.: MediComp Press, 1972.

Romanucci-Ross, L., D.E. Moerman, and L.R. Tancredi, eds. *The Anthropology of Medicine from Culture to Method,* 3d ed. Santa Barbara, Calif.: Greenwood Publishing, 1997.

Rudgley, Richard. *The Alchemy of Culture: Intoxicants in Society.* London: British Museum Press, 1993.

Rudgley, Richard. *The Encyclopedia of Psychoactive Substances.* London: Little, Brown & Company, 1998.

Schlosser, Eric. *Reefer Madness: Sex, Drugs, and Cheap Labor in the American Black Market.* New York: Houghton Mifflin, 2003.

Simpson, B.B., and M. Conner-Ogorzaly. *Economic Botany: Plants in Our World.* 3d ed. New York: McGraw-Hill, 2001.

Articles

Adams, R. "Marihuana." *Science* 92, 115 (August 9, 1940): 115–119.

Budney, A.J., R.G. Vandrey, J.R. Hughes, J.D. Thostenson, and Z. Bursac. "Comparison of Cannabis and Tobacco Withdrawal: Severity and Contribution to Relapse." *Journal of Substance Abuse Treatment* (March 12, 2008).

Hashibe, M., H. Morgenstern, and Y. Cui, et al. "Marijuana Use and the Risk of Lung and Upper Aerodigestive Tract Cancers: Results of a Population-based Case-control Study." *Cancer Epidemiology, Biomarkers, and Prevention* 15, 10 (2006): 1829–1834.

Mandavilli, A. "Marijuana Researchers Reach for Pot of Gold." *Nature Medicine* 9, 10 (October 2003): 1227.

McCarberg, B.H., and R.L. Barkin. "The Future of Cannabinoids as Analgesic Agents: A Pharmacologic, Pharmacokinetic, and Pharmacodynamic Overview." *American Journal of Therapeutics* 14, 5 (September–October 2007): 475–483.

Mechoulam, Raphael. "Marihuana Chemistry." *Science* 168, 3936 (June 5, 1970): 1159–1166.

Moore, T.H., S. Zammit, A. Lingford-Hughes, et al. "Cannabis Use and Risk of Psychotic or Affective Mental Health Outcomes: A Systematic Review." *Lancet* 370, 9584 (2007): 319–328.

Murray R.M., P.D. Morrison, C. Henquet, and M. Di Fiorti.. "Cannabis, the Mind and Society: The Hash Realities." *Nature Reviews in Neuroscience* 8,11 (November 2007): 885–895.

Nicoll, Roger A., and Bradley N. Alger. "The Brain's Own Marijuana." *Scientific American* 21, 6 (December 2004): 45–51.

Pertwee, R.G. "Emerging Strategies for Exploiting Cannabinoid Receptor Agonists as Medicines." *British Journal of Pharmacology.* 156, 3 (February 2009): 397–411.

Russo, E. "History of Cannabis and its Preparations in Saga, Science, and Sobriquet." *Chemistry and Biodiversity* 4 (2007): 1614–1646.

Sachse-Seeboth, C., et al. "Interindividual Variation in the Pharmacokinetics of Delta 9-tetrahydrocannabinol as Related to Genetic Polymorphisms in CYP2C9." *Clinical Pharmacology and Therapeutics* 85, 3 (March 2009): 273–276.

Strougo, A., et al. "Modelling of the Concentration-effect Relationship of THC on Central Nervous System Parameters and Heart Rate: Insight into its

Mechanisms of Action and a Tool for Clinical Research and Development of Cannabinoids." *Journal of Psychopharmacology* 22, 7 (September 2008): 717–726.

Vandrey, Ryan, and Margaret Haney. "Pharmacotherapy for Cannabis Dependence: How Close Are We?" *CNS Drugs* 23, 7 (2009): 543–553.

Watts, G. "Science Commentary: Cannabis Confusions." *British Medical Journal* 332 (2006): 175–176.

Web Sites

Office of Applied Studies, Substance Abuse and Mental Health Services Administration
http://www.oas.samhsa.gov

National Clearinghouse for Alcohol and Drug Information
http://csat.samhsa.gov/publications.aspx

StreetDrugs.org
http://streetdrugs.org/

National Institute on Drug Abuse: NIDA for Teens
http://www.teens.drugabuse.gov

National Institute on Drug Abuse: "The Facts About Marijuana"
http://www.marijuana-info.org

National Institute on Drug Abuse InfoFacts: Marijuana
http://www.nida.nih.gov/infofacts/marijuana.html

National Pain Foundation
http://www.nationalpainfoundation.org/articles/112/marijuana-and-pain-management

U.S. Drug Enforcement Agency
http://www.justice.gov/dea/concern/marijuana.html

Office of National Drug Control Policy
http://www.whitehousedrugpolicy.gov/drugfact/marijuana/index.
html

University of California Center for Medical Cannabis Research
http://www.cmcr.ucsd.edu/geninfo/research.htm

Medical Marijuana, Inc.
http://www.medicalmarijuanainc.com

Society for Neuroscience. "Brain Facts"
http://www.sfn.org/index.aspx?pagename=brainfacts

Index

137

About the Author

Brigid M. Kane received her undergraduate degree in biology from Virginia Polytechnic Institute and State University in Blacksburg, Virginia, and her master's degree from Temple University in Philadelphia, where her focus was on cellular and developmental biology. Kane is a science writer working primarily in the fields of infectious diseases, HIV/AIDS, public health, oncology/hematology, and pharmaceutical science. She has authored articles for *Science* and *Annals of Internal Medicine* and has prepared numerous clinical research manuscripts for peer-reviewed medical and scientific journals, as well as continuing education manuscripts and projects for physicians and other health-care professionals. Recent projects have led Kane to explore nonmedical science topics, such as the metallurgy and chemistry of carbon steel.

About the Consulting Editor

Consulting editor **David J. Triggle, Ph.D.,** is a SUNY Distinguished Professor and the University Professor at the State University of New York at Buffalo. These are the two highest academic ranks of the university. Professor Triggle received his education in the United Kingdom with a Ph.D. degree in chemistry at the University of Hull. Following post-doctoral fellowships at the University of Ottawa (Canada) and the University of London (United Kingdom) he assumed a position in the School of Pharmacy at the University at Buffalo. He served as chairman of the Department of Biochemical Pharmacology from 1971 to 1985 and as Dean of the School of Pharmacy from 1985 to 1995. From 1996 to 2001 he served as Dean of the Graduate School and from 1999 to 2001 was also the University Provost. He is currently the University Professor, in which capacity he teaches bioethics and science policy, and is President of the Center for Inquiry Institute, a think tank located in Amherst, New York and devoted to issues around the public understanding of science. In the latter respect he is a major contributor to the online M.Ed. program—"Science and The Public"—in the Graduate School of Education and The Center for Inquiry.